## CURRENT ISSUES BIBLE STUDY SERIES

# Faith and
# Pop Culture

## CHRISTIANITY TODAY

INTERNATIONAL

## THOMAS NELSON

*Since 1798*

NASHVILLE   DALLAS   MEXICO CITY   RIO DE JANEIRO   BEIJING

3/17/10

Jonathan & Michelle — Damian's friends
having baby Friday

Liz — brother Daniel in
Afghanistan

Nate — dad home & doing well
Allison receiving
prayer for need for care
ministry at new campus

Linda — studying Bible seriously &
God uses in
accountability

Natalie —

Bob — financial wisdom,
sticking to God's plan &
discipline

John — Jacob's visit with
John's parents

Mario — praise that Jackson
Dusart doing well —
ongoing heart health

# OTHER BOOKS IN THIS SERIES

Editor: Kelli B. Trujillo
Development Editors: Kelli B. Trujillo and Roxanne Wieman
Associate Editor: JoHannah Reardon
Review Editor: David Neff
Page Designer: Robin Crosslin

ISBN 13: 978-1418534097

*Printed in the United States of America*
09 10 11 12 RRD 5 4 3 2

# CONTENTS

4/7/10

~ Damian's friend -
~ John - job/unemployed
~ Bob - allergies / new
             campus
                 involvement

~ Duane ~ traveling
              home from Georgia

        ~ quality
           quiet time

~ Linda & Nate ~ appointment
                    in Maryland

           ~ fertility doctor

~ healthy expectations
     about new campus

~ Tim & brother Dave
         who has cancer / not a
                           Christian

        ~ Tim visiting in Texas

# CONTRIBUTING WRITERS

**Bryan Belknap** is a screenwriter, author, and speaker living in Los Angeles.

**Chris Blumhofer** is associate editor of BuildingChurchLeaders.com, a website devoted to equipping church leaders.

**Lee Eclov** is senior pastor of Village Church of Lincolnshire, Illinois.

**Todd Hertz** is managing editor of Christianity Today International's *Ignite Your Faith* magazine.

**LeAnne Benfield Martin** is a writer who lives in Georgia.

**Eric Miller** is associate professor of history at Geneva College.

**Sam O'Neal** is managing editor of SmallGroups.com, a Christianity Today International online resource.

**Jeffrey Overstreet** is a movie critic whose reviews and articles can be found at LookingCloser.org and on ChristianityTodayMovies.com. He is the author of *Through a Screen Darkly: Looking Closer at Beauty, Truth, and Evil in the Movies* and *Auralia's Colors*.

**Jennifer Merri Parker** is a professional Christian writer, editor, teacher and speaker.

**Thomas Purifoy, Jr.,** is a writer, producer, and director living in Nashville, Tennessee, who has taught small-group Bible studies and Sunday school classes for more than fifteen years. His latest film-based Bible study curriculum is called Modern Parables (see http://modernparable.com).

**Rosalie de Rosset** is a professor of English, literature, and homiletics at Moody Bible Institute in Chicago.

**Mark Storer** is a writer and teacher in Camarillo, California.

**Kelli B. Trujillo** is a writer, editor, and adult ministry leader at her church in Indianapolis.

**Kyle White** is the founding director of Neighbors' House, a ministry to at-risk students in DeKalb, Illinois. He is a freelance writer and blogger (see KyleLWhite.blogspot.com).

**Richard Winter** is professor of practical theology and head of the counseling program at Covenant Theological Seminary; he is the author of several books including *Still Bored in a Culture of Entertainment: Rediscovering Passion and Wonder.*

# INTRODUCTION

In some parts of the world, it is a rare luxury to be enjoyed perhaps once or twice a year. But here in America it is viewed as a foundational aspect of everyday life. *It* is entertainment—a source of much joy and also much consternation for growing Christians. Without it, many of us would feel lost . . . adrift . . . and, let's be honest here, just plain bored.

From movies to TV to sports to books to video games, we spend a lot of time and energy entertaining ourselves. And along with the relaxation, the laughs, and the inspiration we can gain from these experiences also come dangers: temptation, frivolity, self-centered living, and more. In these studies you'll wrestle with the positive, negative, and neutral aspects of entertainment and the place it should have in the life of a Christian.

This *Current Issues Bible Study* is designed to facilitate lively and engaging discussion on various facets of entertainment and how it connects to our lives as Jesus's followers. As you explore this topic together, we hope this guide will help you grow closer as a group and challenge you in ways you may not expect.

## For Small Groups

These studies are designed to be used in small groups—communities of people with a commitment to and connection with each other. Whether you're an existing small group or you're just planning to meet for the next eight weeks, this resource will help you deepen your personal faith and grow closer with each other.

Along with the eight studies, you'll find a bonus Small-Group Builder article from Christianity Today's SmallGroups.com. On SmallGroups.com, you'll find everything you need to successfully run a small-groups ministry. The insightful, free articles and theme-specific downloads provide expert training. The reproducible curriculum courses bring thought leaders from across the world into your group's discussion at a fraction of the price. And the revolutionary SmallGroupsConnect social network will help keep your group organized and connected 24/7.

### *Christianity Today* **Articles**

Each study session begins with one or two thought-provoking articles from *Christianity Today* or one of its sister publications. These articles are meant to help you dive deeply into the topic and engage with a variety of thoughts and opinions. Be sure to read the articles before you arrive to your small group meeting; the time you invest on the front end will greatly enrich your group's discussion. As you read, you may find the articles persuasive and agree heartily with their conclusions; other times you may disagree with the claims of an article, but that's great too. We want these articles to serve as a springboard for lively discussion, so differences in opinion are welcome. For more insightful articles from *Christianity Today* magazine, visit http://www.ctlibrary.com/ and subscribe now.

## Timing

These studies are designed to be flexible, with plenty of discussion, activities, and prayer time to fill a full small group meeting. If you'd like, you can zero in on a few questions or teaching points and discuss them in greater depth, or you can aim to spend a few minutes on each question of a given session. Be sure to manage your time so that you're able to spend time on the "Going Forward" questions and prayer time at the end of each study.

## Ground Rules

True spiritual growth happens in the context of a vibrant Christian community. To establish that type of community in your small group, we recommend a few *ground rules*.

- *Guarantee confidentiality*. Promise together that whatever is said in the context of your small group meeting is kept there. This sense of trust and safety will enable you to more honestly share your spiritual struggles.

- *Participate—with balance*. We all have different personalities. Some of us like to talk . . . a lot. Others of us prefer to be quiet. But for this study to truly benefit your group, everyone needs to participate. Make it a personal goal to answer (aloud) at least half of the discussion questions in a given session. This will allow space for others to talk (lest you dominate discussion too much) but will also guarantee your own contribution is made to the discussion (from which other group members will benefit).

• *Be an attentive listener—to each other and to God.* As you read Scripture and discuss these important cultural issues, focus with care and love on the other members of your group. These questions are designed to be open-ended and to allow for a diversity of opinion. Be gracious toward others who express views that are different than your own. And even more important, prayerfully remain attentive to the presence of God speaking to and guiding your group through the Holy Spirit.

It is our prayer that this *Current Issues Bible Study* will change the lives of your group members as you seek to integrate your faith into the cultural issues you face every day. May the Holy Spirit work in and through your group as you challenge and encourage each other in spiritual growth.

Are movies the art form of our day? And if so, how do they connect with Christian faith?

Genesis 1:20–31

Exodus 35:30–35

Psalm 19:1–6

# DA VINCI, VAN GOGH, MONET, AND . . . *ROCKY*?

■

For as long as the church has existed, Christians have embraced the arts as a poignant and effective method for telling the story of the Bible. Using visual displays, music, and literature, no organization has been more responsible than the church for commissioning and appreciating artists and their craft. Ironically, no organization has been more responsible than the church for suppressing (and even persecuting) the artists and art forms it deems inappropriate.

So, what is a proper relationship between the church and the arts? How has that relationship changed in recent generations? Using the *Christianity Today* article "Modernity's Art Form" this study addresses these questions and more about Christians and their interaction with modern forms of art, like movies.

## ■ Before You Meet

Read "Modernity's Art Form" from *Christianity Today*.

# MODERNITY'S ART FORM

### A lush guide to film through Christian eyes.
### A Review of Jeffrey Overstreet's book *Through a Screen Darkly*

*by Eric Miller*

Just in time for the Oscars, Jeffrey Overstreet treats us to a warm, even lush guide to film through Christian eyes. He weaves deft plot description and personal narrative into what he describes as "an invitation to journey." As a mainstay of *Christianity Today*'s movies website (christianitytoday.com/movies) and the beneficiary of evangelical Protestant schooling from kindergarten through his college years, Overstreet knows his audience well. He confesses "a strange compulsion to sit down between Christian culture and secular society, trying to help them understand each other—and ultimately God—better through a shared experience of art." In this book, his voice speaks to the Christian side of that divide, even as his eyes are lit up by the other.

Overstreet's memoirist-as-mentor tack serves the "invitation" part of the book well, enabling him to address contentious issues from an intimate, personal vantage. Nudity, sex, violence, profanity, anti-Christian storylines: he approaches each in a seasoned, sometimes battle-weary way, still smarting from the e-mail shellackings he's received from hostile readers over the years. So in the form of a story—his own story—he responds, seeking to deepen the reader's notion of what art is and fashion a new framework for considering the vexing questions art invariably raises.

Overstreet is most convincing in his effort to show evangelical readers that their traditional approach to art tends to impede both a rich experience of the goodness of God and a profound understanding of this present darkness. "If I think that by withdrawing I can get away from sin's influence in the world, I forget that sin is active within my own walls and within my own heart," he writes. He urges readers instead to more daringly embrace good art, whether Christian or not, as a means of expanding vision and enlarging wisdom, accepting "the sensual pleasure of God's gifts" even as they take care to avoid the kind of exposure that may actually diminish their ability to taste goodness.

To this end, Overstreet gives layers of description of dozens of films, ranging from *The Empire Strikes Back* to *Taxi Driver* to *Wings of Desire*. It's a clinic in art criticism. Through his earnest and illuminating instruction, we learn much about genre, sacramentality, cinematography, and more. His quest to "apprehend beauty wherever I can find it" is clearly an impassioned romance, one he longs to usher us into as well.

### Dangerous Romance

But romance, however beautiful, is also dangerous, as anyone over fifteen knows well. Its promise can be realized only if one manages to remain tough-minded and softhearted at once, the steep but sure pathway to maturity. This is the direction Overstreet seeks to lead us in, and toward that end two questions arise.

Does film as a medium deserve our easy embrace? Nothing could be more natural for most of us than watching a movie—all the more reason to hold this unusually forceful, relatively new, quite unnatural art form up to scrutiny. Its ability to instantly captivate is unparalleled in the history of art. One illustration: when silent film star Rudolph Valentino died suddenly in 1926, tens of thousands lined the streets of New York; several women attempted suicide. Why? What are the mysterious but powerful effects of film (and other electronic media) on the self?

This leads to the second question: what is film's place in the larger story of modernity—with its scientistic faith, its atomizing ideals, its technology-suffused fantasies, and its violent despair, each so decisively affecting the church, the world, and the earth itself? Art criticism is sharpest when it is nested within a broader, deeper cultural criticism: a systematically developed understanding of a people that exposes and reveals the nature of the times. Film, as the quintessentially modern art form, is part of a monumental moment in time whose meaning Christians must insistently probe if we are to evade the wiles of the age and reach toward it with redeeming strength.

Overstreet's achievement in this book is his winsome articulation of the magnificence of art and its irreplaceable part in a fully human life. With an enlarging vision of the story in which our art has unfolded, his criticism will cut through our enigmatic darkness with yet more light.

*Eric Miller is associate professor of history at Geneva College. "Modernity's Art Form" was first published in* Christianity Today, *February 2007, Vol. 51, No. 2.*

# ■ Open Up

Select one of these activities to launch your discussion time.

## Option 1

Discuss these icebreaker questions:

- What's your favorite form of entertainment (such as movies, TV, video games, books, and so on)? Why?

- When have you been uplifted, encouraged, or inspired by a movie or another work of art? Why?

- Can you think of a time when a movie or work of art depressed, discouraged, or scandalized you? Describe your experience.

## Option 2

First, take a moment to each jot down three to five movies you'd put on your personal "greatest movies of all time" list.

Once everyone's written down a few ideas, look online together at some film critics' lists of the greatest movies of all time. You can find links to many well-respected lists at www.filmsite.org/films.html. Also look at lists of top-grossing films. You can find this at www.imdb.com/boxoffice/alltimegross or www.filmsite.org/boxoffice.html. (Alternately, a group member can print out copies of the lists before the meeting.)

Review the lists and talk about these questions together:

- Which of the critics' "greatest movies" have you seen? Do you agree that these movies are classics?

- Compare the list of films considered to be good art (greatest films list) with the list of most popular films (highest grossing list). What stands out to you as the main differences between these films? In general, which list better matches your own taste in movies?

- How do these movie choices compare or contrast with the movies you wrote down?

## ■ The Issue

Over the past fifty years, few experiences have been more universal to American culture than a trip to the movies. Most of us can recall the excitement of sitting down in front of that big screen, popcorn in hand, waiting for the lights to dim and the music to begin.

Why do we go to the movies? Sometimes we go as an avenue of "escape" from the stress of everyday life. At other times, though, we have much deeper reasons for the entertainment we pursue. In his book *Reel Spirituality: Theology and Film in Dialogue*, Fuller Theological Seminary professor Robert Johnston writes,

> Movies have, at times, a sacramental capacity to provide the viewer an experience of transcendence. . . . Garrison Keillor once remarked: "If you can't go to church and, for at least a moment, be given transcendence; if you can't go to church and pass briefly from this life into the next; then I can't see why anyone should go. Just a brief moment of transcendence causes you to come out of church a changed person." Commenting on this observation, [Christian author] Ken Gire writes, "I have experienced what Garrison Keillor described more in movie theaters than I have in churches."

- Can you relate to Ken Gire's comment? Describe a time when you've experienced transcendence while watching a movie.

- When you watch movies, do you most often see them as art, education, entertainment, or escape? Or do these categories overlap for you? Explain.

## ■ Reflect

Take a moment to read Genesis 1:20–31, Exodus 35:30–35, and Psalm 19:1–6 on your own. Write down your own observations about the passages: What words, phrases, or images stand out to you most? What insights do these passages give you about the place of art and entertainment in a Christian's life? What questions do these passages bring up?

## ■ Let's Explore

### God is the original creator of beauty and truth.

Read Genesis 1:20–31.

In September of 2006, researchers at Baylor University released a study looking into Americans' different views of God. They uncovered four distinct views of God's personality and interaction with the world: the Authoritarian God, the Benevolent God, the Critical God, and the Distant God. But none of the four represent the first glimpse we get of God in the Bible: the Creative God.

- What does it mean that God described each element of creation as "good"? Why is this important?

- As the creator of all things (including beauty, truth, and art itself), God can rightly be described as the first artist. Does this affect the way you view his character? Your relationship with him? Your view of yourself? Explain.

Read Psalm 19:1–6.

The Bible says that all of God's creation reflects his glory back to him—in essence, all of creation worships its Creator. This includes human beings. However, because we are made in the image of God, we also have the ability to create in our own way. And so our creations, including our various forms of art, have the potential to reflect God's glory as an act of worship.

- The author of "Modernity's Art Form" implies that Christians should view art as "a rich experience of the goodness of God and a profound understanding of this present darkness." What do you think of this statement?

- Which movies or other works of art can you cite that provided such an experience?

- Can art only represent an act of worship on the part of the artist, or could appreciating a work of art also serve as an act of worship to God? In other words, is it possible that watching a movie could result in a worship experience with God? Why or why not?

*Passion of the Christ*

**As followers of God, Christians are called to reflect his beauty and truth to the world through artistic creation or appreciation of the arts.**

Read Exodus 35:30–35.

Bezalel and Oholiab were dedicated followers of God who had been specifically gifted "with skill, ability, and knowledge in all kinds of crafts—to make artistic designs for work in gold, silver, and bronze, to cut and set stones, to work in wood and to engage in all kinds of artistic craftsmanship." These gifts came from the Spirit of God—the same Spirit who blesses others with the gifts of evangelism, prophecy, hospitality, and so on.

That being the case, it is clear that Christians should not abandon artistic expression. In fact, it's surprising that very few Western church groups and denominations place an emphasis on worshiping God through the creation and appreciation of art.

*Blindside*

*Schindler's List*

- Bezalel and Oholiab were gifted in working with gold, silver, bronze, precious stones, and wood. In what ways do today's artists work with the same materials? What are some other materials that modern artists employ?

- In the article, Overstreet is quoted as being on a quest to "apprehend beauty wherever I can find it." Is this a quest that all Christians should participate in, or only those with artistic gifts? In what ways could this type of quest strengthen our relationship with God?

While the arts have traditionally been part of the church throughout its history, there has also always been a tension between the arts and the church, particularly when artistic expressions have been seen as pushing against the bounds of morality. The challenge contemporary Christians face in determining how to navigate issues like nudity or sexuality in films is not a new problem; it's been faced by the church for centuries in the areas of visual and literary art. In "Modernity's Art Form," Eric Miller asks a question that could relate to many forms of art: "Does film deserve our easy embrace?"

- What's your gut reaction to this question? Should the church "embrace" the movies? Why or why not?

C.S. Lewis once wrote about the effect of art (in literature), saying:

We seek enlargement of our being. We want to be more than ourselves. Each of us by nature sees the whole world from one point of view with a perspective and a selectiveness peculiar to himself . . . But we want to escape the illusions of perspective on higher levels too. We want to see with other eyes, to imagine with other imaginations, to feel with other hearts, as well as with our own. (*An Experiment in Criticism*)

Overstreet views films much as Lewis approached literature. In *Through a Screen Darkly* Overstreet urges readers "to more daringly embrace good art, whether Christian or not, as a means of expanding vision and enlarging wisdom."

But film critic Sarah Barnett bemoans the fact that often it's not art or enriching entertainment that motivates us to see films. She writes, "Unfortunately, 'entertainment' has lost its real meaning and has come to mean escapism. Once upon a time, entertainment was more about switching one's mind on than switching it off."

- Describe a specific movie or scene that has expanded your vision, enlarged your wisdom, or switched your mind on. How did that experience of good art enrich your faith?

- Often when Christians talk about the standards they set for watching movies, evaluating a film's moral content is the top priority. But what about setting one's standards according to a film's artistic quality instead? What might that look like?

## ■ Going Forward

In his book *Through a Screen Darkly*, Overstreet shares his desire to "sit down between Christian culture and secular society, trying to help them understand each other—and ultimately God—better through a shared experience of art."

- In what ways can modern art forms, like movies, serve as a common ground between Christian culture and secular society? Share examples of times you've found common ground with non-Christians via the movies.

In *Christianity Today's* Film Forum discussion of movies as art, critic Doug Cummings said:

I think good art can point people toward God in appreciation of Truth and Beauty. I think it's the task of Christian artists to "offer their bodies as living sacrifices" in the creation of art through worship and it's the church's task to let them do it. . . . The church can produce and appreciate art through worship in ways that inform and inspire the culture around us.

- How well is your church doing at producing or appreciating art in a manner that impacts the larger culture? Brainstorm together: what *could* your church do?

- What might you do personally to better integrate your entertainment choices and your Christian understanding of art, beauty, and truth?

Conclude by praying together, focusing on God's role as artist and creator. Seek wisdom together regarding movies and other forms of entertainment. Ask God for guidance in your own creative pursuits. Worship God for the way he's communicated truth and beauty to you through movies or other forms of art.

**Bonus Idea:** At some point in the next week, think of a movie that you would describe as good art—one that inspired and uplifted you, one that is good and noble and pure and true. Rent that movie and watch it. Keep an eye out for chances to apprehend beauty and truth wherever you can find them. Allow yourself to participate in the art of the film, and see if you can direct your appreciation of the experience into a time of meaningful worship.

# ■ Notes

How can great books pave

the road to faith?

**SCRIPTURE FOCUS**

Matthew 13:34–35

Luke 18:1–18

Acts 17:22–31

# WHEN LITERATURE
# LEADS US TO GOD

■

Maybe you're the kind of person who falls asleep
nightly with a novel in hand. Or perhaps the last time
you "read" a book was when you snored through high
school English class. Whether you're a bibliophile, a self-
proclaimed non-reader, or you land somewhere in between,
reading as a form of cultural entertainment is a topic worth
considering. Is literature a spiritually neutral topic or does
it have significance in the life of faith? How does literature
impact our culture? How can it affect our own lives?

High school English teacher Mark Storer says his road
to faith was paved with great literature. He is so convinced
of the power of great reading to change one's life that
he says, "Reading led me to Christ." Great writers,
ancient and contemporary, secular and Christian, in
their honest vision and with their gift of words, keep
taking him back to the Bible and to Christ. In this
study we'll consider if God's truth can be found
in literature, even the secular kind.

## ■ Before You Meet

Read "The Good News According to Twain, Steinbeck, and Dickens" by Mark Storer from *Christianity Today*.

# THE GOOD NEWS ACCORDING TO TWAIN, STEINBECK, AND DICKENS

My road to faith was paved with great literature.

*by Mark Storer*

"It does sometimes seem a shame that Noah and his party did not miss the boat," quips Mark Twain as his sharp tongue aims at the heart of humanity. My favorite thing that Mark Twain satirically advocated, however, was to bring home missionaries from China. He wanted them to "sivilize" Southern white men who had sworn allegiance to the Ku Klux Klan. "You (missionaries) convert roughly one Chinaman per missionary per annum. That is an uphill fight against thirty-three thousand pagans born every day." At such moments, Twain makes me think about Jesus.

But he isn't the only one. In fact, reading led me to Christ. I did not have a conversion experience. No drugs or alcohol sank me to rock bottom. I had no one mentor to lead me to church and ultimately to Christ. The Lord did not call me in a dream or speak in my ear. My faith in Jesus grew over time. I don't think I ever didn't believe in God. From the time I was born, I was brought up in the Protestant church, and while various of my family members traveled far and wide on spiritual journeys, I never did. But I read. I read a great deal.

After a short stint working in radio, I became a teacher and a writer. Soon the books I taught my students began to take hold of me—books I'd known since the time I was in high school were now my own personal Bible of sorts. I taught John Steinbeck's *The Grapes of Wrath* and found that I looked forward to it almost as much as my students loathed it. Reading a book of five-hundred-plus pages is usually not an event anticipated with glee. But as a teacher, I did find joy in it, and what's more, I found God in it.

## Steinbeck's "Jesus"

Steinbeck, who was not known for devout Christian faith, wrote about it all the time. In *The Grapes of Wrath* the secondary character, Jim Casy (note the initials JC, I always tell my students), is an itinerant preacher who has fallen away from the mainstream church. "Just Jim Casy now. Ain't got the call no more. Got a lot of sinful idears—but they seem kinda sensible." Casy is confused and in his confusion he says, "I went off alone and sat and figured. The sperit's strong in me, on'y it ain't the same. I ain't so sure of a lot of things." The tension between human mind and spirit—our desire to do what pleases God and upon trying, our inability to do so—is laid bare here.

Casy's death is even more allegorical than his life. In an attempt to stop farm owners from driving down wages, he leads some of the migrant workers on a strike and tries to force a settlement. It doesn't work, of course, and in a moment of violence remarkable for its sparse telling, Casy is killed. He is standing in a stream of clear water as a flashlight from one of the men chasing him falls on his face. He turns to the man and says, "Listen . . . You fellas don' know what you're doin'. You're helpin' to starve kids." And with that the man, armed with a pick handle, hammers across Casy's cheek and brow. He lays in the stream, lifeless, the flashlight beaming on him. Steinbeck merely dramatized what the Bible has said all along: God is on the side of the downtrodden.

Perhaps no one "secular" author has contributed so much to the Christian faith as Charles Dickens. His novella, *A Christmas Carol*, is perhaps single-handedly responsible for making Christmas a household celebration, as well as a pagan celebration. But in light of his stories of redemption, salvation, and grace, he can be forgiven and perhaps even lauded for bringing Christmas out of the basement of the Western conscience and moving it into the living room.

It is not Ebenezer Scrooge who fascinated me most, though. It is Sydney Carton, the debauched, drunken, and brilliant lawyer from *A Tale of Two Cities* who finds that his sacrifice will redeem him and save his dear friends. It is Carton who, though morose and depressed, drunk and slovenly, gives his life in the uncanny twist of events that lead him to the guillotine in revolutionary Paris.

"I am the resurrection and the life," Sydney keeps hearing over and over again. As his captors prepare to execute him, in the midst of his own sacrifice, he comforts another, a young lady, accused by the "citizens" of France of treason. Sydney tells her to keep her eyes on him. He remains a constant and steady source of hope and inspiration for her. Yet the ridiculous events that lead these two innocents to be executed are not the focus of Dickens's attention. He does not write, in his extraordinary verbosity, about the injustice of the system. Rather, he writes about compassion, healing, understanding, justice, and ultimately faith.

An aside: in the high school where I teach, *A Tale of Two Cities* is core literature for the ninth grade. I am always puzzled when I hear cries about how God has been kicked out of our classrooms. Have those leveling this charge looked at the reading list of their local high schools recently?

In any event, Dickens, more than most classic authors, brought me to Christ. Though not my favorite writer, Dickens unabashedly writes about humanity in a way that would embarrass a twenty-first-century psychologist. As Harvard professor Robert Coles has said, "And Dickens, oh my, what Dickens knew about human nature!"

I am inclined to agree. In *Soul Survivor* Philip Yancey writes of Coles' being drawn to great authors—including Dickens, Flannery O'Connor, Leo Tolstoy, Simone Weil, and William Carlos Williams—while he was a student at Harvard. Like Coles, I have found that these authors are simply retelling the Bible, albeit sometimes in a way that makes some Christians angry. But Coles never blinks. He explains to Yancey that the Bible has all along steadfastly preached that we have both sides in us. We have the ability to be evil and ignorant, and we have the ability to behave with grace and compassion. All of us have those tendencies, and the authors that moved Coles merely repeat that refrain and seek ways for the most despicable of people to be redeemed.

### Beauty, Grace, Power

In the dying days of winter, I teach a book by Zora Neale Hurston called *Their Eyes Were Watching God*. The main character, Janie, is constantly in the spring of her life. Through a series of failed marriages and abusive situations, Janie does not shrink from her circumstances. Rather, she embraces them and lives joyously in God's shadow. "Ev'rybody got to go to God for theyselves," says Janie, speaking from experience. Never cowed or demeaned by her situation, she is an indomitable woman and ultimately finds her own soul. As one of my students wrote in a paper about the book, "Spring is the soul-chasing season." What a tribute to Hurston: she reaches into the black experience in America, and rather than coming out discouraged, as she has every right to do, she finds reason for joy and love.

One line reads, "Dawn and doom were in the branches." Hurston also knew that human beings have the potential for both. Dawn and doom exist in each one of us, and it is up to us to choose which one will succeed. Perhaps this is the ultimate expression of free will that we are given. This is the free will that allows human beings to suffer or alleviate suffering, to love or to hate, to choose spirit over ignorance, compassion over mistrust, and finally to accept and share what there is of living.

In that vein, I have continued to teach. I teach not because I know how to reach students. I teach because they reach me. In the depths of all that is rampant in a high school—drugs, abuse, sexual promiscuity, ignorance, hatred—literature also exists, and with it, God. Ralph Waldo Emerson speaks to students about self-reliance and the power of nature. He speaks to them about losing yourself in order to find yourself. Shakespeare provides such profound glimpses into the human heart that many doubt he could have written them on his own. The beauty of his words, the grace with which he writes, and the power of the human soul and spirit they convey are unmatched in the English language.

Tolkein, Lewis, Frost, and even more contemporary authors like David Guterson, Charles Frasier, Annie Dillard, and Anne Lamott are what led me back to the Bible and to Christ. In their writings is the constant search and an acceptance of sorts that, while we all sin and fall short of the glory of God, we must strive toward that glory while giving love and compassion to those around us. This is not an epiphany or a moment of clarity. This is a lifetime of struggling with answers that belie their questions. It is a terrible honesty and, finally, a hope that God will indeed dwell within us. What a dreadful and wonderful lesson to learn.

---

*Mark Storer is a writer and teacher in Camarillo, California. "The Good News According to Twain, Steinbeck, and Dickens" was first published online* Christianity Today *April 22, 2002.*

## ■ Open Up

Select one of these activities to launch your discussion time.

### Option 1

Discuss these icebreaker questions:

- What do you most often read—fiction, poetry, essays, the news, articles, biography, history? Why does that genre interest you?

- Who is your favorite author or what is your favorite book? Describe why this author or book stands out to you.

### Option 2

Imagine you're writing a book—any type of book you'd like. On a scrap of paper, write down the book's title and a short, one-sentence summary of the plot. What you write can be serious and sincere or funny and completely nonsensical. Write whatever you'd like, but just be sure to keep what you've written a secret (and don't put your name on it)!

When everyone's done, fold up the scraps of paper and put them in a bowl. One at a time, pull out a paper (make sure it's not yours) and read it aloud. Try to guess whose "book" you've drawn. (If you aren't able to guess correctly in a few tries, invite the rest of the group to join in on the guessing.)

## ■ The Issue

In his article "The Good News According to Twain, Steinbeck, and Dickens," English teacher Mark Storer proposes that great literature, whether written from a Christian or secular perspective, can play a pivotal role in a person's understanding of God and the human condition. Storer concludes his article with this commentary on his own journey of faith:

> Tolkein, Lewis, Frost, and even more contemporary authors like David Guterson, Charles Frasier, Annie Dillard, and Anne Lamott are what led me back to the Bible and to Christ. In their writings is the constant

search, and an acceptance of sorts that, while we all sin and fall short of the glory of God, we must strive toward that glory while giving love and compassion to those around us. This is not an epiphany or a moment of clarity. This is a lifetime of struggling with answers that belie their questions. It is a terrible honesty and, finally, a hope that God will indeed dwell within us. What a dreadful and wonderful lesson to learn.

• When has a work of fiction spoken to you about the meaning of life or about God? Share an example (even if it's from your freshman year of high school!).

• How would you define great literature? What do you think marks the kind of great reading Storer describes?

## ■ Reflect

Read Matthew 13:34–35; Luke 18:1–18; and Acts 17:22–31 on your own. Take notes about the words, themes, and ideas that stand out to you. How might these passages relate to the topic of literature? What questions do you have?

## ■ Let's Explore

**God chose to portray his truth not only through explicit facts but also through narrative and stories.**

- What are your favorite Bible stories? Describe what you love about the "characters" and the "plots."

While the Bible does not contain an explicit mandate to read literature, it is more literary than didactic. It does not present theological outlines. In fact, some critics note that Christianity is the most literary religion in the world. In addition to the Bible's varied and colorful stories about nations and individuals, it also contains poetry, drama, visions, and letters. The parables of Jesus—stories that convey truths about God and people and life—grip its readers in ways facts and principles told directly would not.

Read Luke 18:1–8.

- Why do you think Jesus used a story to get his point across in this passage rather than a sermon or explanation?

- Can you feel the difference between being on the receiving end of a pointing finger versus a story? Share an example from your own life of the effect one of these types of experiences (finger-pointing lecture or compelling story) had on you.

Read Matthew 13:34–35.

Jesus frequently told stories in lieu of preaching sermons or as powerful illustrations of his teaching points. In fact, Dudley Nichols, an American screenwriter, once said:

> Jesus of Nazareth could have chosen simply to express Himself in moral precepts; but like a great poet He chose the form of the parable, wonderful short stories that entertained and clothed the moral precept in an eternal form. It is not sufficient to catch man's mind, you must also catch the imaginative faculties of his mind.

Through his storytelling, Jesus provides a model for teaching and learning, demonstrating that spiritual concepts are best remembered when placed in the context of human drama.

- What are some other examples of Jesus's stories that powerfully communicate truth? How do the stories speak to you? (Flip through Matthew, Mark, Luke, and John to get ideas.)

- What part do you think imagination plays in Christianity's expression and practice?

Our lives are full of moral and spiritual choices, the drama of which constitutes great writing. In his article Storer shows how great stories, well told, bring us back to the Bible. Dickens's knowledge of human nature leads the reader repeatedly to recognition of evil, the need for compassion, and the hope and reality of redemption. Instead of pointing a finger at us and saying, "You should do this and that," Dickens introduces us to Ebenezer Scrooge in *The Christmas Carol*, and we see for ourselves the consequences of selfishness and experience the hope of change.

### Truth is always from God—wherever it is found.

- Think about the books (or fictional stories in films or other media) that have deeply connected with you or spoken to you in some way. What truths about life or the human experience did those works of fiction communicate? Share examples.

- Are your favorite books mostly written by Christian authors or by secular authors? Does it matter to you personally if those whose work you read do not profess faith in Jesus Christ? Why or why not?

Although we are fallen, God's image remains in us, providing the basis for our creative gifts and vision. God's saving grace touches the world through the influence of Christian beliefs and values. The ability to write vividly and eloquently is a function of the creative imagination. Even those who do not profess faith in Christ may keenly observe the world if they are endowed with the common grace of powerful imagination. They, too, may create three-dimensional characters who show us something about ourselves, others, and God. Since those gifts—imagination, perception, keen intellect—are given by God, we can enjoy them and learn from them.

Read Acts 17:22–31.

In his sermon delivered on the Areopagus (Greek for "Mars Hill") in Athens, Paul shows he understands his audience and his culture, including its best writers, poets, and philosophers (Epicureans and Stoics in particular). Areopagus was the name of both the hill and the court that met on it. The court was very likely exclusive, commentators say. It was made up of only thirty members, who dealt with cases that ranged from homicide to public morals. There Paul was called upon to state his faith. He spoke compellingly. Referring to secular poets to support his contention that we are created by God, he quotes from the poets twice in one verse: "By his power we think and move and exist," and, "We are his children" (v. 28).

- How important do you think it is to understand the culture around you? How do you personally go about gaining a better understanding of your culture?

- Like Paul did, we can use the great literature of our culture to point out truths about God in our conversations with non-Christians. Think of a novel or poem you've read that was full of truth which could be used to make a Christian point to a non-Christian friend. What truths or tough questions about life could that book or poem help you discuss?

## ■ Going Forward

According to a landmark study by the National Endowment for the Arts, fewer than half of American adults read literature—and the percentage who read is continuing to decline.

- Why do you think that is? Are you satisfied with the amount of time you personally devote to reading—or would you like to read more? Explain.

Take a moment to privately and silently consider these questions about your own reading habits:

- How does what you read challenge your thinking? (Or is it usually what many people call "a quick read"?)

- How do the books you read build links to the greatest book of all?

- Is there a work of literature that you've been planning to or wanting to read but haven't gotten around to it yet? If so, write it here and consider starting it this week:

_____

Gather back together to pray as a group, praising God as the Author of life and the master Storyteller who revealed mysteries of the universe through parables and stories.

If applicable, talk with each other about your reading plans; consider reading and discussing a great book together as a group or in pairs. For ideas of where to start, consider some of the books and authors mentioned by Storer in his article or review the suggestions of pastor and writer Eugene Peterson in his book *Take and Read: Spiritual Reading: An Annotated List* (Eerdmans).

# Do we take sports seriously enough?

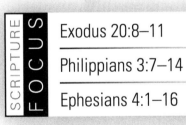

| SCRIPTURE FOCUS | |
| --- | --- |
| | Exodus 20:8–11 |
| | Philippians 3:7–14 |
| | Ephesians 4:1–16 |

# FINDING GOD IN SPORTS

■

Come on! Steroids. NBA players in and out of jail. Dads tackling kids on the peewee football field. Beer commercials. NFL salaries. Sports have become way too important in our culture. What's the point anymore?

What if sports were meant to be more than just a guilty pleasure. In "The Lost Joy of Sports," the editors of *Christianity Today* propose: "The problem is that we no longer take sports seriously enough." This discussion guide will help you look at the point behind sports in God's economy. How are serious sports meant to reflect discipleship, community, and even Sabbath?

## ■ Before You Meet

Read "The Lost Joy of Sports" from *Christianity Today*.

# THE LOST JOY OF SPORTS

### Sports is much more important than our culture lets on.

*A Christianity Today editorial*

Where there is sport, there is scandal. The latest examples, all from fall 2004: Football phenom Terrell Owens and sultry starlet Nicollette Sheridan glorified illicit sex in a pre-game network teaser. Baseball stars Jason Giambi and Barry Bonds (of the New York Yankees and the San Francisco Giants, respectively) admitted they illegally used performance-enhancing steroids. And there was that professional fight (the Detroit Pistons vs. the Indiana Pacers), at which a basketball game finally broke out—after Piston Ron Artest, among others, was pulled from the stands while punching out a fan.

The problems of sports run long and wide. One well-known writer has said, "Television threatens to engulf many of the inherent values of sports," and "Throughout our sports programs there is an undue emphasis on violence." Another book summarizes the problem of modern American sports culture: "cheating, rule violations, ego exaggeration."

There is nothing new under the sports sun. The first two quotes come from James Michener's *Sports in America*, written nearly thirty years ago. The last quote is from Tony Ladd's and James A. Mathiesen's *Muscular Christianity* (1999), and goes on to note that these problems "came to fruition in the 1920s and affected sport for the remainder of the twentieth century." And the first part of the next century, we might add.

As Paul put it in Romans 1, too many professional athletes are "filled with all manner of unrighteousness, evil, covetousness, malice. They are . . . insolent, haughty, boastful, inventors of evil . . . foolish, faithless, heartless, ruthless." Okay, he wasn't talking about athletes but idolaters. Unfortunately, too often the shoe fits.

The temptation for Christians is to drone on that things have gotten out of hand, that sports is a waste of time at best and is a form of idolatry at worst, that winning has became too important, that we take sports way too seriously.

We beg to differ. The problem is that we no longer take sports seriously enough.

## Signal of Transcendence

Sports is supposed to be a form of play. Catholic scholar Johan Huizinga, in his classic *Homo Ludens*, said play is "a free activity standing quite consciously outside ordinary life as being 'not serious,' but at the same time absorbing the play intensely and utterly. . . . It proceeds within its own proper boundaries of time and space according to fixed rules and in an orderly manner."

The great Green Bay Packers coach (and amateur Catholic theologian), Vince Lombardi, put it well: "Winning isn't everything, it's the only thing." This doesn't mean "win at any cost," or "do anything to win," because play proceeds "according to fixed rules and in an orderly manner." But when one is absorbed in play "intensely and utterly," the game will be played as if winning is "the only thing"—as if there is really nothing more important in the world at that moment than the game itself.

This type of play, one that fully absorbs our attention and joy, is, according to scholar Michael Novak, "the first act of freedom. . . . The first free act of the human is to assign limits within which freedom can be at play. Play is not tied to necessity, except to the necessity of the human spirit to exercise its freedom, to enjoy something that is not practical, or productive, or required for gaining food or shelter." Or multimillion dollar contracts.

In other words, it is play precisely because it is, in respect to our day-to-day lives, pointless. Like the Sabbath—a day in which nothing useful (by human reckoning) gets done. The Sabbath is not merely an occasion to rest from labor, to get ready for another blistering week of work—as if God thought up the Sabbath because, exhausted after six overtime days, he was just too pooped to go on. Instead, the Sabbath is the seventh and final act of creation, the culmination of Creation—the point of it all.

The Latin Vulgate translation of the Bible, the church's only version for one thousand years, translated Proverbs 8:30–31 like this: "I [Wisdom] was at his side putting together everything, my delight increasing each day, playing before him all the while, playing in this world made of dust and my delight was to be with the sons of men." Wisdom in this passage has been commonly seen as a reference to Christ, the Word. After reflecting on this passage, medieval theologian Thomas Aquinas concluded, as one scholar summed it up, "God plays. God creates playing. And man should play if he is to live as humanly as possible and to know reality, since it is created by God's playfulness."

Perhaps liberties were taken with some Hebrew words here, but Aquinas's point is more than amply illustrated in the sweep of salvation history, which begins with the creation of the Sabbath and culminates with the Eternal Sabbath. Whenever we take a Sabbath, as a day or as an activity in the midst of a day, we proclaim this fundamental truth of existence. This is why Peter Berger, in his *Rumor of Angels*, notes that play is a "signal of transcendence."

But from Little League to the Super Bowl, we often see the very opposite of play. We have traded play's freedom and joy for pottage that is merely useful: money (from college scholarships to gaudy professional riches), sex (increasingly a part of the package of professional sports), and power (or, more precisely, cultural status).

How exactly we retrieve the freedom and joy of sports is a complex matter. But Christians have a crucial voice in our ongoing cultural conversations that take place from children's leagues to professional sports. It is not a voice that whines that sports is "just a game" but one that demands that we take sports as seriously as possible, as if it were play.

*"The Lost Joy of Sports,"* Christianity Today *editorial available at* ChristianBibleStudies.com.

# ■ Open Up

Select one of these activities to launch your discussion time.

## Option 1

To add some fun to the discussion, each group member should wear a jersey, T-shirt, special colors, or other costume (such as athletic gear) to represent your favorite sport, team, or athlete. Use your outfit to help explain your answers to these icebreaker questions.

- Good, bad, or ugly, what's been your sports experience? Would you rather play or watch sports? Why?

- Who's your favorite team or athlete? Why?

- What was your favorite sports moment in which you participated? Or, alternately, what's a favorite sports moment you saw on TV or in person? Why?

## Option 2

As a group, watch an inspiring scene from a great sports-themed movie such as *Chariots of Fire, We Are Marshall, Remember the Titans, Rudy, The Cutting Edge, Rocky, Hoosiers,* or *The Rookie.* (Need help finding a scene? Look for the big game, the final race or match, or the tie-breaking score scene in these movies—you'll be sure to find a tear-jerkingly inspiring clip!)

Talk about these questions:

- When have you been inspired by an athlete?

- In what ways does sport bring out the "best" in humanity? Share an example.

- How does the modern sports world also draw out the "worst"? Give examples you've seen or read about.

# ■ The Issue

There is the story of Super Bowl XLI, where African-American coaches Tony Dungy and Lovie Smith were able to use the game as a platform to highlight the gospel and the issue of race in America. There is the story of the Iraqi national soccer team—including Sunnis, Shi'ites, and Kurds—working together to win the 2007 Asian Cup. And then there is, uh, well . . . it seems we have to dig pretty deep to come up with positive stories to justify our love affair with sports.

But are sports more than just a guilty pleasure or an arena for pride and egotism? The *Christianity Today* editorial "The Lost Joy of Sports" posits that the problem isn't "that we take sports way too seriously. . . . The problem is that we no longer take sports seriously enough."

The editors write that sport is a "signal of transcendence." Hmm, perhaps you never thought that while watching the Chicago Bears. But sport, like any form of play, reflects freedom—a rising above the day-to-day toil to something more. Sabbath. Rest. God's ultimate desire for his creation. Freedom to be intently and intensely human. In sports we can experience and communicate something akin to Sabbath. And that is serious business, since God Almighty created and modeled Sabbath for us as "the culmination of Creation—the point of it all." Perhaps we have missed all the good that sports can reflect, like Sabbath, discipleship, and community.

- What value do you think God puts on sports? Explain your point of view.

- Friendly competition can quickly turn cruel; supporting one's team can easily turn into idolatry. How do you navigate the issues of competition and idolatry when it comes to sports and your faith?

## ■ Reflect

Take a moment to read Exodus 20:8–11; Philippians 3:7–14; and Ephesians 4:1–16 on your own. Jot down a few notes and observations about these passages: In what ways do these teachings relate to the articles you read? What questions do these passages bring up for you? What are the key ideas that stand out to you?

## ■ Let's Explore

### Serious sport reflects Sabbath.

Sabbath is one of those uneasy concepts in our faith. We all know that we should value it, honor it, and observe a Sabbath rest. But how? Is it okay to watch or play sports? Or to engage in other activities? Our questions may be evidence that we are missing the point. The *Christianity Today* editorial points out: "The Sabbath is not merely an occasion to rest from labor . . . as if God thought up the Sabbath because, exhausted after six overtime days, he was just too pooped to go on. Instead, the Sabbath is the seventh and final act of creation, the culmination . . . the point of it all." Thus, Sabbath is time for freedom, to play, to enjoy, to rest. Does our observation of Sabbath and sport reflect that joy?

- What's your favorite thing to do on a Sunday afternoon? Do you think it's okay to watch or play sports on Sunday, the Sabbath? Why or why not?

Read Exodus 20:8–11. The word *holy* means "set apart." The Sabbath sets apart, honors, and celebrates the good, finished work of God in creation. And it points ahead to the "rest" that Christ accomplishes, or finishes, for us in his redemptive work on the Cross. Further, it points to the culmination of all things, as we enter a heavenly Sabbath rest (Hebrews 4:1–11). This is a blessed and holy day indeed!

- What do you think it looks like to "keep the Sabbath holy"? Has your picture of this changed as you've grown in faith? Explain.

- "The Sabbath is the seventh and final act of creation, the culmination . . . the point of it all," the CT editorial claims. What do you think that means? How could this truth affect your workweek? Your play?

- In what ways do you think play, and sport specifically, reflect the concept of Sabbath? Does your play and participation in sports reflect that? Explain.

## Serious sport reflects discipleship.

Legendary coach Vince Lombardi said, "The price of success is hard work, dedication to the job at hand, and the determination that whether we win or lose, we have applied the best of ourselves to the task at hand." This sounds a lot like discipleship. Following and becoming more like Jesus requires a singular focus. Another legendary coach, the apostle Paul, wrote, "Forgetting the past and straining toward what is ahead, I keep trying to reach the goal and get the prize for which God called me through Christ to the life above" (Philippians 3:13–14). Serious sport includes focus, training, and finishing well—a reflection of discipleship.

- In terms of athletics, what are some images of *endurance* that come to mind for you? Who are specific athletes or what are some particular sports that you think exemplify endurance? (If you are an athlete, share about a sport or event that really tested your endurance.)

Read Philippians 3:7–14.

- In what ways is the Christian life like a race? What are some other ways Christian discipleship correlates to sports imagery?

- Why would Paul need to write this part of his letter to the church at Philippi? In what ways does this passage come as an encouragement to you right now? As a rebuke?

**Serious sport reflects community.**

Everyone's heard the coach's adage "There is no 'I' in *team*." To which smart-alecky kids always reply, "But there is 'M-E'!" There is also no 'I' in *church*. Scripture even describes the church as a body—with individual believers as body parts—to show its unity. The church moves together to accomplish its kingdom work. Serious sports can give us a glimpse of the unity of the body of Christ. Babe Ruth, one of the first players to be elected to the Baseball Hall of Fame, said, "The way a team plays as a whole determines its success. You may have the greatest bunch of individual stars in the world, but if they don't play together, the club won't be worth a dime."

- What's the best team you've ever been a part of? Why?

- In his book *Playing with God,* author William J. Baker quotes a high school girl's track coach. She says, in part, regarding coaching, "I'm here to show my own kids that sharing your talents with others is valuable, even when it's not easy" [p. 260]. What is the value of sharing your talents in sports? In the church?

Read Ephesians 4:1–16.

- What gifts have you been given by Christ to build up his body? (Ask your small group if you are not sure.) How do you use them?

- How is your church or small group like a team (or a body)? How do you play well together? In what ways do you need some coaching on the concept of "team"?

# ■ Going Forward

- How do you think a Christian should define and exemplify good sportsmanship? Where should we draw the line between healthy competitive behavior in sports and mean-spirited or un-Christlike behavior done in the name of competition? Share personal examples.

Amazingly, we may not be serious enough about sports in our culture. Nothing in God's creation is wasted. Even play points to the heart of God. And sport can reflect discipleship, community, even Sabbath rest. Thus, as Christians, we look for opportunities to play intently and intensely, and to reflect his joy to others.

- In light of this view of play, how can we begin to redeem sports in our viewing and in our participation? How can you use sport and play to reflect Christ's love toward others?

Pray together, thanking God for the pleasures of sport and play and dedicating yourselves to run the race of faith together with determination and endurance.

## Bonus Ideas

You may want to consider using sport as an avenue for community-building or service as a group. Here are three ideas:

- As a small group, postpone your regular meeting agenda and find an active game you can all play together. Depending on your group, play volleyball, kickball, or bocce ball. Don't worry if there's not much talent; just steer clear of dodge ball! Take on another small group if you can and whip their pants (in brotherly love, of course)! Afterward, grab something to drink and discuss how you played together, what you learned about each other, and what the freedom of play showed you about God and Sabbath.

- As a small group, consider training for a 5K run. There are probably a few right around your community for good causes. A 5K (3.1 miles) is long enough to be challenging but short enough to be doable. It would be a good community builder as you work toward a goal together. When you finish the run, celebrate!

• Commit to become coaches for local youth sports teams. You don't need to be an expert. In fact, sponsor and coach a team as a small group (everyone can pitch in, from coaching to providing halftime snacks to designing t-shirts to planning the end-of-season celebration). Further, consider sponsoring a team from a low-income apartment complex where funds and other necessary resources may be lacking. It sounds like a big commitment, but some sports, like YMCA flag football, only have a six-week season. What a way to be a neighbor by building community, teaching sportsmanship, and generally loving kids. Who knows what God will do with those relationships!

With hundreds of channels

screaming for our attention,

how do we decide what—

or whether—to watch?

SCRIPTURE FOCUS

1 Corinthians 9:19–23,
10:23–33

# THE TELEVISION

# DILEMMA

■

TV poses a difficult challenge for most believers. Is TV-watching just harmless fun? Should we indulge in hours upon hours of "mindless" entertainment? Or should we only watch clean, uplifting, family-friendly shows? Or is the solution simply to take a sledgehammer to the TV screen and then toss it out in next week's recycling bin?

In this study we'll examine two very different responses to the TV dilemma as two Christian writers "debate" the pros and cons of television. Jennifer Merri Parker is a self-confessed "media brat." Like most Americans, she grew up watching a lot of television—and still does watch quite a bit. Some people, on the other hand, consider television "a destroyer" and have removed it from their lives entirely.

What's the best approach to television? This study will help you consider your TV viewing from a biblical perspective.

# ■ Before You Meet

Read "Why You'll Never Get Me to Turn on TV" by Jennifer Merri Parker.

# WHY YOU'LL NEVER GET ME TO TURN ON TV

*by Jennifer Merri Parker*

Boob tube. Idiot box. Couch potato fertilizer. Whatever you want to call it, TV is here to stay, at least until the next big technological innovation. Whether you consider the revolutionary invention a blessing or a curse, it's difficult to arrange your life so as to avoid its influence. . . . You can run but you can't hide. You can turn it off, but those pixels continue to stream through the air.

And frankly, I'm glad they do.

I must confess that I sometimes grow impatient with people who did not grow up watching television. They force me to break up the flow of images and allusions in my speech, because I must stop again and again to ask, "Did you ever see . . . ?" Talking with them is an exercise in cross-cultural communication.

With these people I have to force myself to avoid jokes or quotes that require knowledge of TV shows that I consider cultural icons. I have to explain the difference between the Munsters and the Addams Family, or to compare and contrast the Jeffersons, the Evanses (of *Good Times*), and the Huxstables (*The Cosby Show*) for someone who doesn't understand the socioeconomic nuances involved. Because we don't share the context, my metaphors get strangled, and my communication is, if not severely hampered, at least rendered less colorful and lively.

The point is that I am a media brat. I grew up watching—and still watch—a lot of television. Deep in the lush jungle of my brain, along with the Jungian archetypes, the Greek, Roman, and Norse mythological figures, and other ideas furnished by a western education, live Captain Kirk and Uhura, Ginger and Mary Ann, and a host of other characters, images, and scenarios from three decades of network TV viewing. With these figures informing my thoughts, "Promethean" and "Gilliganesque" are equally valid adjectives.

In most contexts, this works well, since most of the people I encounter watch a lot of television too. At work, on the subway, at the doctor's office, I can utter a Homer Simpson "Doh!" when I make a mistake or say "I'm going to pull a MacGyver" when I have to improvise. Nods and smiles of recognition greet me, because TV-speak is a common tongue across America and other parts of the world. Television enables people who do not have common geographies, histories, or mythologies to engage in communication. It gives us a primer full of stories and characters that we can use as a basis for friendly exchange.

Whether this is a good or a bad situation I won't argue. It is a fact of postmodern life in America. Ours is a media-driven culture, and the medium of greatest reach and influence, at least for the moment, is television. Many Christians see it as a challenge, an object for reclamation, to be redeemed by creating positive-value programming to leaven the lump. Others see TV as an unregenerate tool of the devil, its applications for education, outreach, and evangelism notwithstanding. I'm afraid I don't fall squarely into either camp. I simply believe it is my sacred duty to watch as much TV as I can without neglecting other obligations.

Some people think that a writer should hate television for displacing the printed word in popularity and importance, and for discouraging children (and adults) from reading books. I'm not convinced that television does this simply by offering an attractive alternative, but even so, all's fair. I don't just tolerate this medium. I love it. In it I find insights, fresh ideas, and new inspiration to inform my own work of fiction, poetry, and non-fiction writing.

I know few writers, and fewer Christians, who share my devotion. In fact, some of my favorite writers have maligned television. In *Walking on Water*, author Madeleine L'Engle expresses disdain for the medium. "Creative involvement: that's the basic difference between reading a book and watching TV," she writes. "In watching TV we are passive; sponges; we do nothing."

As much as I love and respect L'Engle, I beg to differ. There is nothing inherently magic or hypnotic about television that forces people to turn off their brains, suspend their will and reason, or lie prostrate at the mercy of violent, materialistic, and immoral propaganda. Viewers need not accept everything they see on television any more than they need to believe everything they read. When we watch television, high-speed information in visual, aural, and sometimes subliminal form rushes at us, and our brains get busy absorbing, interpreting, cataloguing, and selecting.

The fact that we often watch TV sitting or lying down, in silence, and without conscious effort does not mean that what we are doing involves no exercise of intellect. We may joke about "couch potatoes," but advertisers do not market to vegetables. They develop commercials based on the premise that viewers will see, hear, consider, and eventually act on what they have seen and heard. They are not responsible for how intelligently we weigh the "evidence" of our eyes and ears, but they count on our ability to make choices.

And so should we. Consciously and conscientiously, we should choose not only what programs to view, but how to think about and react to what we are viewing. There is nothing we cannot watch safely and profitably if we watch with critical awareness of all the levels on which TV engages the mind.

This is not to suggest that I approve of all or even most of what is shown on television. My taste runs a fairly eclectic gamut, but I lean slightly toward fictional comedy, drama, and biography, as opposed to news, music, documentary, and arts programs. I will watch almost anything that tells someone's story well. Whether the characters are real or fictional, as long as their story feels authentic and can teach me something about the human experience (admittedly these are broad and subjective criteria), I am likely to sit for thirty minutes to two hours at a time, letting the story do its work on me. Simultaneously, my mind goes to work on the story, probing for resonance with my own experience, credibility of language and action, similarity to or difference from other stories, humor, applicability, value, meaning, truth. In other words, as I watch I sit in judgment, and this is mental work, as surely as poring over a chapter of Dickens is work.

Granted, much of what is on television today is less than worthwhile. Some of it is downright damaging, in terms of the immorality depicted, the seriousness trivialized, and the stupidity glorified. If this is the common culture that television fosters, many ask, why should we want to take part in its conversation? Shouldn't we protect ourselves and our children from the river of garbage relentlessly pouring from the television screens?

These are valid questions, but taking our children or ourselves out of the loop doesn't destroy the loop. Being voluntarily uninformed, even of evil, is at best a temporary, and at worst a false protection. Of course, television, like any other fact of life, should be introduced to children carefully, with thoughtful deliberation as to how early and how much to expose them to it. It is too easy simply to forbid an activity rather than to monitor it, make judgments, and set boundaries concerning it, and sift through what in it is good, bad, or possibly instructive. As much as I agree that parents should forbid their children to watch certain shows, I also insist that parents should choose certain shows to allow, or even to watch with their children. Teaching kids to be critical viewers is as smart as giving them swimming lessons.

Adults need to monitor their own TV watching with as much vigilance as they would use for their children. I don't pretend that filling one's spirit with a steady dose of violence, lasciviousness, or ribald joking isn't going to have an effect. Philippians 4 is never more applicable than when one has the remote in hand. We should mine the airwaves for the best of what TV has to offer of what is true, pure, and honest. And even when we view the cynical realism of popular adult dramas, or the tragi-comic aspects of human frailty depicted in news and documentary programs, we should look for transcendent meaning and incarnational characters in their stories, just as we would seek them out in the chance encounters of our lives. To quote L'Engle again, "There is nothing so secular that it cannot be sacred, and that is one of the deepest messages of the Incarnation."

The greatest danger with TV is its use as a substitute for human interaction; it is easy to make up for a lack of fulfilling relationships by turning on TV's artificial presence. Worse yet, some use the TV for its noise value; it becomes a means to avoid the much needed spiritual exercise of silence. When viewing habits begin to affect one's prayer life or personal relationships, it is time to go on a tele-fast.

All in all, though, I consider it a great blessing to have the continuous stream of stories on TV from which to draw information and inspiration. I am grateful for my legacy as a media brat, which gives me a language for thinking about and communicating with my culture, and for initiating conversations with strangers who are bound to me across time and space by this unique medium.

I am even grateful for the mixture of treasures and trash that flows to us TV watchers over the airwaves. It gives us a chance to practice "rightly dividing." Separating the great truths from the gross trivia is wonderful exercise for the Christian intellect. Just think, a rigorous workout, without ever leaving the sofa.

*Jennifer Merri Parker is a professional Christian writer/editor, teacher and speaker.*

## ■ Open Up

Select one of these activities to launch your discussion time.

### Option 1

Discuss these icebreaker questions by completing each sentence:

- I like watching TV because . . . (or I *don't* like watching TV because . . .)
- I draw the line at watching . . .
- I know I've been watching too much TV when . . .

### Option 2

Take a moment to each privately write down a TV show you enjoyed watching or have memories of seeing during these stages of your life:

Early childhood:

Elementary-school or preteen years:

Teenage years:

Young adulthood:

The present:

Now, as a group create a large timeline on a sheet of paper or poster board with each of these life stages on it, like so:

| Early childhood | Pre-teen | Teenage | Young adult | Present |

Share with each other what you wrote down and list everyone's TV shows under each life stage on the timeline. Discuss the similarities and differences you see between the various TV shows selected. Then talk about these questions:

- Do the shows you chose reveal anything about who you are or what your interests are? Share an example.

- Do you think watching TV has had a formative affect on your life? If so, would you say that effect was positive or negative? Explain.

## ■ The Issue

According to some reports, Americans have their TVs on an average of eight hours a day.

- Why do you think people watch *so much* TV? Brainstorm together some of the reasons (positive, negative, or neutral) that you think drive people to watch television.

Whether you're in the eight-hours-a-day boat or you just watch, say, *five* hours per diem, we all know TV can be a discourteous guest in our homes. For most Christians, this issue is a challenge. In her article, Jennifer Parker highlights some of the difficulties Christians face in the world of TV while still asserting that TV can be a positive and enjoyable part of one's life.

Some of you, though, may choose to keep TV entirely out of your life.

- Which viewpoint best reflects your own perspective on this issue? Share a quote or idea from an article that particularly resonated with you.

# ■ Reflect

Take a moment on your own to read 1 Corinthians 9:19–23 and 10:23–33. Jot down a few notes and observations about the passages: What are the key ideas in these passages? How might they relate to the issue of television? What questions do these passages raise for you?

# ■ Let's Explore

### We are called to connect with others, but is speaking the cultural language of TV a necessary means of doing so?

- Can you imagine your life without any television? What might you gain from such a lifestyle? What might you lose?

In her article, Parker observes, "Whether this is a good or a bad situation I won't argue. It is a fact of postmodern life in America. Ours is a media-driven culture, and the medium of greatest reach and influence, at least for the moment, is television." And because it is part of our culture, watching television allows us to converse with others in the same "cultural language" as those around us.

Not only was there no television in Bible times, but there was little entertainment of any kind. Those living in the Greek world had more entertainment options than those in Palestine at the time of Christ, but the

Bible doesn't directly address how Christians should interact with, say, the Greek theater. So we have to evaluate our viewing habits by broader biblical attitudes.

Read 1 Corinthians 9:19–23. Here, the apostle Paul expresses his passion for sharing the Good News and his willingness to "become all things to all people" for that purpose. This passage is often used to support the idea of Christians seeking to be culturally relevant in order to evangelize. (People also cite passages such as Paul's dialogue in Athens in Acts 17:16–34.)

- Do you think this passage supports the idea of Christians today being culturally relevant in areas like media choices, appearance, and other social habits in order to relate to non-Christians? Or is that interpretation taking Paul's words too far out of context? Explain.

- Paul is clear that his motivation here is to share the Good News. When has a television show played a part in your efforts to reach out to and share Christ with non-Christians? Share an example, such as a friendship growing because of a common connection or a time when an issue or character in a TV show opened the door to discuss more meaningful issues.

**Christians should not ignore the dangers that come with television viewing.**

Though some people disagree on their approach to television, they *do* agree that some television content poses serious problems. Parker summarizes the danger this way: "[M]uch of what is on television today is less than worthwhile. Some of it is downright damaging, in terms of the immorality depicted, the seriousness trivialized, and the stupidity glorified."

- Think of the most recent time you watched television: what did you see in a show or in advertisements that was immoral, stupid, or that trivialized a serious matter (such as sex, violence, or faith)? Share specific examples.

- Based on what you've read in Scripture or learned in church, do you believe there are things on TV that are absolutely off-limits for Christians? Explain.

Read 1 Corinthians 10:23–33. In this passage Paul was helping Christians sort out matters of liberty and responsibility when it came to eating food sacrificed to idols. In verse 23, when he wrote "We are allowed to do all things," he was probably quoting a slogan used by Christians in the Corinthian church who got carried away with their Christian liberty. Paul quoted it, then tempered it.

- Not everything in this passage transfers to a discussion of TV viewing, but what are some transferable principles you see here? Give examples of how these principles could relate to choices about television viewing.

- Do you think a person can watch a TV show "for the glory of God"? How would this be different than watching a show merely for one's own entertainment? How would applying 1 Corinthians 10:31 to your TV-viewing change your habits?

Beyond the blatantly obvious problems with some TV content, Parker notes that TV-viewing shouldn't replace human relationships or drown out time with God.

- As a group, make a list of reasons or arguments why TV-viewing can be harmful. Do you think TV-viewing has any redemptive features?

How does this list challenge you personally?

## ■ Going Forward

Form pairs to read and discuss the text below.

How can you discern what you should or shouldn't watch on TV? Consider these three "tests" that may help you discern what you should or shouldn't watch on television:

1. *The test of conscience.* Romans 14 and 1 Corinthians 10 address the subject of Christian liberty versus responsibility to others. Romans 14:22b says, "Blessed is the man who does not condemn himself by what he approves" (NIV). One simple test of what you can watch is how your conscience reacts to it. Ask yourself: Do I feel guilty about what I've seen? To do something you feel guilty about, even if it doesn't seem to bother another Christian, is an act of disobedience for you. If

you feel guilty, you must think God disapproves. Even if you should come to a conclusion later that he doesn't, to do now what you feel displeases God is to foster rebellion against God's will.

2. *Aggravating your weaknesses.* Matthew 13:22 points out how the "worries about this life and the temptation of wealth" can choke a person's faith. TV can help those thorns grow. There are many things on TV that aggravate our personal weaknesses and drain our faith. Watching the news, for example, is rarely wrong, but some people, especially during a major crisis, can become news junkies. That may fuel a pervasive anxiety that denies what the Bible teaches us about God's sovereignty and care. Or simply watching too much TV—whatever the content—may keep us from loving our family as we should or doing work we need to do. In such a case, the content isn't the problem; the time squandered is.

3. *Smudging your view of God.* In the Beatitudes Jesus said, "They are blessed whose thoughts are pure, for they will see God" (Matt. 5:8). The pervasive worldliness of television can gradually smudge our spiritual sight, the way eyeglasses pick up dust and smudges unnoticed by the person wearing them. While nothing we watch may be terrible, all that inane comedy, green-eyed commercials, gruesome cop shows, or earth-bound love stories can smudge our view of God until we can no longer pray in faith (if we pray at all), nor worship adoringly, nor serve wholeheartedly; all because we no longer see God clearly.

- Which "test" from the box above do you most need to incorporate into your thinking about TV viewing? Why?

- What are some small steps you can take to help bring your TV viewing under the Lord's control? Think of at least one specific limit you will set or step you plan to take and share it with your partner.

Pray in pairs about the ways you've felt challenged by God during this discussion, asking for wisdom and commitment to respond to God's leading in your life and in your media choices.

Must all entertainment Christians enjoy be "family friendly"?

SCRIPTURE FOCUS

Philippians 4:8

Ephesians 5:1–20

# COVER YOUR EYES!

■

Ah, the cherished list of prohibitions: don't drink, don't smoke, and don't go out with girls who do. The unofficial fourth item on this list would undoubtedly be: don't go to movies. (Or, if your Grammie was feisty, she'd qualify "rated-R movies.")

Too bad Grammie never contended with thirty screens at the multi-plex, 150 cable channels, and movies streaming on the Web or downloaded to your iPod and cell phone! How can one discern when it's safe to open one's eyes, especially when films with undeniably Christian messages like *The Passion of the Christ*, *Changing Lanes*, and *Dead Man Walking* boast an R-rating? Where on earth does a Christian draw the line on what they watch?

This study will look at how to deal with questionable (or outright bad) content on TV or film. We will read the *Christianity Today* article "Have We Lost Our Minds?" by Jeffrey Overstreet in which he responds to the complaints of readers who question his judgment when commending films with questionable content.

## ■ Before You Meet

Read "Have We Lost Our Minds?" by Jeffrey Overstreet from ChristianityTodayMovies.com.

> *CT Movies (part of Christianity Today International) has a clear mission statement, which includes "informing and equipping Christian moviegoers to make discerning choices about films through timely coverage, insightful reviews and interviews, educated opinion, and relevant news—all from a biblical worldview." A number of readers—including some media personalities—have raised some questions about CT Movies' coverage, especially in the wake of our annual best-of-the-year lists, which often include some films that are not "family friendly." One of CT Movies' film critics, Jeffrey Overstreet, has written the following commentary, partly in response to some of these questions, and partly to explain his personal philosophy of reviewing movies.*

# HAVE WE LOST OUR MINDS?

### How can Christian movie critics say good things about films with questionable content—and give poor reviews to "Christian" movies?

*by Jeffrey Overstreet*

Has Christianity Today Movies gone off the deep end when it includes R-rated—and decidedly non-family-friendly—films in its best-of-the-year lists? Are we missing something when we give good reviews to movies that depict sinful behavior—or when we give less-than-stellar reviews to "Christian" films?

Have we lost our minds?

And so go some of the questions we sometimes get from readers. They're good questions, and they deserve an answer.

I'll start by saying that all of us writing reviews for CT Movies are Christians, desiring to glorify Christ with our writing, and determined to write the best film reviews we can.

Other CT Movies critics can speak for themselves. But as for me, my review writing is:

- driven by a desire to celebrate excellence, because excellence reflects God's glory. (And that means I want to highlight it and celebrate it wherever I find it, even in the work of people who don't realize that their work reaffirms God's truth.)

- driven by a desire to expose mediocrity and encourage artists to higher standards, in order to better reflect God's glory and honor him.

- driven by a hunger for more storytelling and art-making that is challenging, compelling, transcendent, even life-changing.

- driven by a dissatisfaction with, and weariness of, works that are simplistic, or sentimental, or manipulative, or preachy, or that misrepresent the world we live in.

- driven by a respect for "Sunday school lesson" storytelling, but also by a compelling desire to grow from "milk" to "meat." Sermons have their proper place and purpose, but *art* is something different. I want to encourage audiences to move beyond simplistic, formulaic gospel lessons into the magnificence of the gospel as it is revealed in the lives of our neighbors, in creation, in history, in aesthetics, in mystery, and in the darkest corners of human experience.

- driven by dissatisfaction with work that just "preaches to the choir" or that wraps up messages we already accept in packages that are cheap and derivative.

**Applauding Evil on the Big Screen?**

While I acknowledge that artists must often reflect back to us the world in all of its ugliness, portraying the vulgar behaviors of human beings like you and me and our neighbors, I do not praise portrayals that condone, glorify, or recommend vulgar behavior.

Instead, I acknowledge and respect portrayals that expose wickedness and invite us to consider the reality of evil and the consequences of wrongdoing. If those things are shown in context, and shown in a way that contributes to the meaningful whole, that is a rewarding pursuit that glorifies God. ("Have nothing to do with the unfruitful deeds of darkness," says Paul in Ephesians 5:11. "Instead, even expose them.")

If portrayals of evil in a film are merely indulgent or excessive or employed just to hold our attention, I strive to warn viewers about that in my review. Such recklessness wastes our time and abuses our imaginations. It's flat-out irresponsible.

The great Christian artist Flannery O'Connor spoke out clearly on this point, saying that great art includes nothing gratuitous or indulgent or unnecessary. And, taking a note from stories in Scripture, she was not afraid to include portrayals of grotesque human behavior in her storytelling. (Many Christians today would probably call her work "vulgar," when in fact it is about vulgarity.)

I want to see that what is good is lifted up. And I want to see crass and sinful behavior reflected truthfully so that we can see it as unhealthy and then live our lives with that understanding.

In other words, I am looking for signs of truth, beauty, excellence, and redemption in art. And that means looking closer, not putting on blinders.

## Holding Fast to What Is Good

To "test all things, and hold fast to what is good"—to borrow a phrase from a letter to the Thessalonians—that is a high calling, and a difficult challenge. I am still learning how to do it.

As I grow, I move farther away from the prevalent sentiment of my conservative Christian upbringing—"In the name of Jesus, be nice." Christians who strive to glorify God with excellence need to have thick skins, humbly setting aside their ego for the sake of learning how they can improve their work. Movies—especially "Christian movies"—should not be excused from criticism just because they wear "good messages" on their sleeves. A good message in a bad package is a lousy way to draw others to Christ . . . in fact, it sends people running the other way. Who wants to be part of something that is cheaply made or dishonest about the challenges of this world? Who wants to be told that Jesus will make us happy and successful when Christ promises us that our lives in his service will be filled with hardship and struggle and unanswered questions? Even the great heroes of the faith were plagued by questions and doubt and frustration, and many of their lives were decidedly R-rated stories.

(This goes for reviewers as well. I used to be a hothead if someone criticized my reviews, but I'm learning to value those remarks, to go back and reexamine my opinions, and revise them if necessary. But I still struggle to remain calm if somebody tells me I'm "anti-Christian" merely because I point out weaknesses in a Christian movie.)

If my reviews are going to be part of the way I share Christ with others, they must be honest, truthful, uncompromising, gracious, and willing to admit fault and find virtue in films from anybody, anywhere. Christ is reflected in beauty, goodness, and truth wherever it can be found— including, sometimes, in the R-rated material of secular culture.

Many Christians are not comfortable with art that reflects the complexity and the darkness of the world. Many would prefer movies that make them comfortable, or that steer their attentions away from the problems in the world and the rough edges of worldly people. They prefer movies that tell them that Christians are clearly "the good guys" and everybody else, well, they're the bad guys. And they do not discern the difference between portraying/exposing wickedness and actually *condoning* wickedness.

They want Christian critics to condemn movies that portray the reality of evil, because dealing with evil is a discomforting, painful, sometimes horrifying process. They have accused me of celebrating works that "advance profane causes" rather than considering the truth that I hope they will see in contemporary cinema.

I have not been hired to give four stars to movies that present the gospel simply and clearly. I am here to consider how the film conveys what it conveys, whether there is room for improvement, and whether that vision is truthful and meaningful. My reviews should discuss the technical excellence of each film I consider, whether inspiring or disturbing, and what a film might reveal about good and evil, choices and consequences, humankind and God's designs. That's one way in which film critics fulfill their responsibility to "test all things and hold fast to what is good."

## Flawed Humans, Flawed Films

All art, even the greatest art, will be flawed in some way because art is the work of flawed human beings. Likewise, all art, especially great art, will reflect something of God, because all of us have "eternity in our hearts." As C. S. Lewis observed, we do not create, but rather, we arrange elements that God has made and put them in a frame. Those elements "pour forth speech" as God intended, even when our own agendas interrupt or dilute that speech.

I anticipate that films made by people who aren't Christians will reflect "worldly" ideas and values, and as they do, I point that out. But I am not here to serve as a judge or to approach their work with a "search and destroy" mentality. In examining a movie, whether it's *Pan's Labyrinth* or *Lassie* or *L'Enfant* or *Little Miss Sunshine* . . . or *Facing the Giants* . . . it is my responsibility to point out weaknesses, but also strengths, and to do all of this with grace and truth.

Too many Christian media personalities and critics are preoccupied with condemnation, condescension, and "labeling" everything they see. I know this because I behaved this way myself for many years—I railed against movies that offended me, calling them "worldly" or "abhorrent." I was so focused on finding a shortlist of items that offended me (cuss words, murders, sexual misbehavior) that I was blind to how these discomforting elements might actually contribute to meaningful art.

Today, I keep this at the front of my mind—Frederick Buechner says, "The world speaks of holy things in the only language it knows, which is a worldly language." If we're going to communicate with our worldly neighbors, we need to know and attend to their language.

Just as Christ approached people with open arms and a listening ear, instead of immediately shouting out their faults in public, we want to approach our neighbors and their movies with grace and attentiveness. (In fact, one of the few times Christ ever loudly and publicly condemned someone, he was responding to religious men who were self-righteously condemning the culture around them. Any Christians who speak about matters of culture and art should take that to heart.)

Too many of the films that have inspired, moved, and ministered to me and my neighbors have been labeled and rejected as "abominations" by those who announce themselves as the voice of the church on these matters. This approach sends messages of arrogance and contempt, when we should be known for our love of beauty, excellence, and the revelation of God in a messy world. No wonder our neighbors shake their heads and roll their eyes when they see a Christian ranting about movies on MSNBC.

### Art Criticism: My Mission and My Passion

I am an evangelical Christian, and I am a film critic. Although it goes against what the world has come to expect from Christian film critics, it is my mission and passion to celebrate the truth and beauty revealed in art from all corners of the world, even from those corners in which Christ is not embraced. I believe that if we accept this mission and develop this passion we will be drawn into a more meaningful and fruitful engagement with our culture, opening more opportunities to highlight the ways in which Christ reveals himself. I call that evangelism.

CT Movies reviewers have been criticized for giving less-than-stellar reviews to movies in which the gospel was clearly presented. We do not object to sharing the gospel. But we are art critics. And good art cannot be reduced to a simple, extractable message. If your movie leads up to a simple "Come to Jesus" climax, that may make for an entertaining sermon but don't ask us to praise it as great storytelling. That's an altar call, not art.

Sermons have their place. I look forward to them every week. But when I go to a movie, I do not want the gospel preached to me. That makes the audience feel cheated, like they've been baited in for a story and then hit with a sales pitch. Only true masters of art are able to weave the clear message of the gospel into something greater than itself . . . a lasting and powerful incarnation.

*Chariots of Fire*, often celebrated as a great "Christian movie," included gospel messages but it did so as part of a much greater ambition. It gave us two complex and compelling character studies—Eric Liddell and Harold Abrahams—and it dared to suggest something even more: that living out the call of the gospel might not be just about preaching; it might be about running at the Olympics, and running with integrity. The craft of whole-hearted running "preached" in a way that a sermon could not.

Francis of Assisi said, "Preach the gospel. When necessary, use words." I love that. It suggests that the gospel is not so much a matter of making your message clear. It's not about ending the film with an evangelistic climax that declares, "The moral of this story is . . ." It is about the form, the beauty, the truth of that artwork.

Some have observed that our reviews sometimes read like "secular" reviews and thus accuse us of writing "non-Christian" reviews. But our reviews are no such thing. Instead:

- We are here to love our neighbors by attending to their art with care and discernment.
- We are here to acknowledge the beauty and ugliness manifest in the world and reflected in art.
- We are here to address our readers with care, making them aware of the nature of the art so that they can decide whether any particular film is worth their own time and attention. (Each viewer is different, faced with different issues of conscience, so we emphasize *discernment*, rather than exhorting people to see things that would draw them into temptation or compromise.)
- And we are here to examine each film, hold fast to what is good and truthful, and expose what is shoddy or false or mediocre or indulgent or unnecessary.

God does not rely solely on Christian artists to reveal himself to the world. From him all things come, through him all things live, and for him all things exist. These days, some of us may encounter him in the Cineplex, even during a Saturday matinee . . . if we go in with minds awake, eyes to see, and ears to hear.

---

*Jeffrey Overstreet is a movie critic and author; you can find his reviews, essays, and more on his Web site www.lookingcloser.org as well as at www.christianitytodaymovies.com. He is the author of* Through a Screen Darkly, *a memoir depicting his adventures in movie-going, and* Auralia's Colors, *the first novel in a four-part fantasy series. "Have We Lost Our Minds?" was published by CT Movies in February 2007 with permission from Jeffrey Overstreet; a longer version of this article was first published on Jeffrey Overstreet's blog, Looking Closer.*

# ■ Open Up

Select one of these activities to launch your discussion time.

## Option 1

Discuss these icebreaker questions:

• What is your favorite movie of all time? Why?

• Is there a movie that you're sometimes ashamed to admit that you love? (For example, you may not want to discuss it in front of your parents or your pastor.) If yes—and if you've got the guts—tell the group what it is and explain why you may feel a bit embarrassed by it.

• Name some movies that Christians have boycotted through the years. How did these boycotts make you feel?

## Option 2

Let's play charades! List some popular films on slips of paper and put them in a bowl.

Form two or more teams, then take turns playing. To play, choose someone on your team to draw a slip of paper from the bowl. Without using any words or sounds, that person must get your team to guess the name of the movie you chose. You'll have one minute to guess each movie title.

# ■ The Issue

Jeffery Overstreet's article "Have We Lost Our Minds?" was written partly in response to comments from readers about a recent CT Movies' Critics' Choice list which included films that contain objectionable content. Readers said things like:

"The devil lives in the extremes. Get back to the cross."

"Your Critics' Choice Awards saddens me. The majority are rated R and PG-13 and so is it any wonder that we are dealing with such immorality in our churches? I can't help but wonder how we pridefully think we can watch hours of sexual content and violence and not have it affect our minds."

"Are you not supposed to be a Christian magazine? What is wrong with you? I will pray God conflicts [convicts] your hearts and opens your eyes."

In his article, Overstreet looks at a provocative question that is significant for all of us as we make decisions about the types of films we watch and enjoy: is it acceptable for Christians to watch movies with questionable content like foul language, violence, nudity, or even portrayals of sexual behavior?

- Focus on the contrasting points of view between the readers who commented above and Christian movie critics like Overstreet. How would you briefly sum up the way people from each camp would answer this question: is it acceptable for Christians to watch movies with questionable content?

- What's your personal gut reaction to Overstreet's article? Explain.

# ■ Reflect

Take a moment to read Philippians 4:8 and Ephesians 5:1–20 on your own. Jot down what stands out to you most about the passages, especially how they might relate to watching movies.

# ■ Let's Explore

### We are to set a high standard for what we do—or do not—watch.

Many Christians use Philippians 4:8 to condemn watching movies, especially those with objectionable content like foul language, violence, or sex. Re-read Philippians 4:8.

- Do you agree with this application of the passage? Should this passage be the guideline on which we base our movie-going decisions? If so, *how* should it serve as a guideline? If not, why not?

- Do you think a film or story can be true, right, or honorable while still containing what some might consider offensive material? If possible, share an example to explain your view.

- Many have posited that if the Bible were portrayed on film exactly as it is written, many parts would deserve an R-rating. Name some scenes or stories from the Bible that might also be considered "objectionable" content if portrayed on a film. How do these types of passages interplay with your understanding of Philippians 4:8?

## Some depictions of evil in film portray a truthful message about the consequences of sin or the effects of sin on humankind.

- Whether it's movies, literature, or paintings, do you agree with the idea that "good art" must honestly depict the world—even its ugly side? Why or why not?

- If a filmmaker or other type of artist depicts only positive, happy things, is it still good art? Or is the quality of the art compromised by its untruthfulness? Share an example to explain your point of view on this issue.

In his article, Overstreet writes:

I acknowledge and respect portrayals that expose wickedness and invite us to consider the reality of evil and the consequences of wrongdoing. If those things are shown in context, and shown in a way that contributes to the meaningful whole, that is a rewarding pursuit that glorifies God. ("Have nothing to do with the unfruitful deeds of darkness," says Paul in Ephesians 5:11. "Instead, even expose them.")

• Do you agree with Overstreet's stance here? If you agree, does this mean we can watch anything? If you disagree, how can you remain salt and light without engaging with the realities of a fallen world? Share examples of movies you've seen that portrayed sin *and* sin's consequences; or, alternately, share examples of movies that glorified sin without honestly depicting sin's consequence.

Overstreet quotes Ephesians 5:11 to make his point. Examine that verse in its context by reviewing Ephesians 5:1–20.

• What does this passage have to say that could apply directly or indirectly to your choices about movies?

- Do you think someone can be an "imitator of God" (Ephesians 5:1, NIV) while watching R-rated films? Why or why not?

**An accurate and honest portrayal of the human experience in film will likely include objectionable content; we each must determine how to respond to such portrayals.**

Many people believe that the criteria for determining the acceptability of a film for Christians rest on both the moral content (sex, language, violence, etc.) and the proclamation of a clear gospel message. David Taylor, Arts Minister for Hope Chapel in Austin, Texas, presents a different view in a CT Movies article "The Honest-to-God Truth About Movies":

> Plenty of folks tend to be only interested in religious stuff—Jesus-stories, end-time prophecies, how-to-stay-a-virgin romantic comedies. But biblically, we're to be interested in everything, even as God is interested in everything. All of life merits comment, and by such comment is made meaningful. Under the gaze of the artist, life really does begin to make a little more sense. So if you're going to make a movie with a message, take advantage of the near infinite possibilities that surround you, like bacteria or turtles, or your uncle.

- How well does this statement line up with your personal opinion on movies?

• How would the idea of allowing your faith to encompass "all of life" affect how you view films? Share an example.

• What positive things might happen if you opened yourself up to a broader range of films? What negative impact might that have on your life?

• What practical things can you do in order to gain a better sense of discernment regarding the movies you choose to watch?

## ■ Going Forward

Form pairs to read and discuss this quote from Jeffrey Overstreet's article:

Movies—especially "Christian movies"—should not be excused from criticism just because they wear "good messages" on their sleeves. A good message in a bad package is a lousy way to draw others to Christ . . . in fact, it sends people running the other way. Who wants to be part of something that is cheaply made or dishonest about the challenges of this world? Who wants to be told that Jesus will make us happy and successful, when Christ promises us that our lives in his service will be filled with hardship and struggle and unanswered questions? Even the great heroes of the faith were plagued by questions and doubt and frustration, and many of their lives were decidedly R-rated stories.

• What's one film you've seen that surprised you by making you think about God or your faith despite the fact it was decidedly non-Christian? On the other hand, has there been a film that you deeply regretted watching?

• What conclusions can you draw from those experiences concerning your faith and its relation to movies?

• How will what you've discussed here change your media choices in the future?

Pray for each other in pairs, asking God's Holy Spirit to convict where he must, provide strength to follow through on what you've learned about watching films, and provide divine guidance every step of the way.

# ■ Notes

Can violence be

entertainment for

Christians?

SCRIPTURE FOCUS

Matthew 5:1–12, 38–48

1 Corinthians 15:20–28

# JESUS AND
# SHOOT 'EM UP

■

The Academy Award for best film of 2007 went to the relentlessly violent and bloody *No Country for Old Men*. What's the film about? In part, it's a lament that our society is spiraling into depravity and violence. We're in an interesting place when we have to shock people with violence in order to talk about the direction of violence in our country!

How, in this atmosphere, do we follow Christ when it comes to violence in media? On the other hand, why might we be drawn to violent films and video games in the first place? The *Christianity Today* editorial "Deadening the Heart" will serve as a jumping off point for this discussion.

## ■ Before You Meet

Read "Deadening the Heart" from *Christianity Today* magazine.

# DEADENING THE HEART

### Killer video games are no "safety valve"—quite the opposite

*A* Christianity Today *editorial*

Steve Johnson, author of *Everything Bad is Good for You*, says violent video games are good for children. He thinks that video games such as *Grand Theft Auto: San Andreas* may "function as a kind of safety valve—they let kids who would otherwise be doing violent things for the thrill of it get out those kind of feelings [while] sitting at home at a screen." Says Johnson: "This may have a deterrent effect on violence."

But the American Psychological Association thinks otherwise. Time spent playing violent video games "increases aggressive thoughts, aggressive behavior, and angry feelings among youth." Less than a week before the *Ottawa Citizen* reported Johnson's remarks, the professional society for psychologists acted on twenty years of research into the effects of violent video games. After a "special committee" reviewed more than seventy studies, the organization adopted a resolution calling for the "reduction of violence in interactive media used by children and adolescents."

APA scholars cited a study of eighth- and ninth-grade teachers. The teachers said that the students who spent time playing violent video games were more hostile than other children and more likely to argue with authority figures and fellow students. And according to another study of six hundred eighth- and ninth-graders, students not normally prone to aggression are nearly ten times as likely to get into a fight after playing a violent video game.

Good teachers know three things that contribute to effective learning: active participation, rehearsing behavioral sequences rather than discrete acts, and repetition, repetition, repetition. Video games employ all three. In addition, the vast majority of the gaming scenarios (like the random killing of prostitutes) fail to show the real-life consequences of violence. Perpetrators go unpunished. In short, violent games can deaden us to the horror of violence and stimulate our native sinfulness. It shouldn't surprise us that all media shapes us, which is one reason Paul exhorts us to think on things that are true, honorable, pure, lovely, commendable, and excellent (Phil. 4).

Some say these are just games and that we shouldn't take them so seriously. But in the wake of the 1998 school-yard massacre in Jonesboro, Arkansas, military expert David Grossman showed CT readers how these games use the same operant conditioning techniques used by armies to overcome recruits' natural aversion to killing.

To be sure, there is a difference in setting—between the home (where real violence is eschewed otherwise) and the military (where the environment reinforces the violence in the video games). Still, it is not hard to see that repeated exposure to random violence can have a detrimental effect.

Others point to the violence found in traditional storytelling, wondering what the difference is. Indeed, fairy tales are often gruesome, with wolves gobbling grandmas and witches baking little children. But such fairy tales are pieces of cathartic moral fiction that help children process their fears. Biblical violence is every bit as gruesome, and it likewise helps us construct a moral universe. Goliath's severed head is not the end of a gory story. It is the beginning of a long saga in which the champion of God's people must struggle with hubris and learn humility.

We support the APA resolution that asks educators to help students apply the same critical viewing skills to violent video games that can be applied to movies and television. This might be a way for youth leaders to engage their charges. Such media literacy programs not only reduce the negative effects of watching violent programming, they reduce the amount of time children watch television. The participatory nature of video games makes this critical-viewing strategy an especially difficult challenge, but outside of a complete ban on games that employ random violence (not politically possible), this is a good first step.

*"Deadening the Heart" was first published in* Christianity Today *October 21, 2005.*

# ■ Open Up

Select one of these activities to launch your discussion time.

## Option 1

Discuss these icebreaker questions:

- Do you like to play video games? If so, what's your favorite and why? If not, explain why.

- What were the standards or rules in your family growing up regarding media (movies, TV, video games)? Did you think they were fair? How about now?

- What's worse in a movie: sex or violence? How did you come up with that answer?

## Option 2

As a group, have your own Academy Awards for movies you've seen this past year. Make a voting sheet as a group using traditional categories like: Best Movie, Best Comedy, Best Drama, Best Actor/Actress, and so on. You can also make up some of your own categories, like: Best Car Chase, Movies I Walked Out On, Best Chick-flick/Guy-movie, and so on.

Once you've zeroed in on a few categories, nominate films, then vote. Have everyone share their voting and reasoning. Afterward discuss this:

- What do you think your movie choices say about you?

- What do these choices say—if anything—about your group's view of violence in movies? What do they reveal about your tolerance of violence?

# ■ The Issue

The *Christianity Today* editorial "Deadening the Heart" takes issue with the idea held by some in our culture that violent video games "may have a deterrent effect on violence" as they let kids take out their aggression on-screen rather than in real life. The CT editors, however, contend that, "Good teachers know three things that contribute to effective learning: active participation, rehearsing behavioral sequences rather than discrete acts, and repetition, repetition, repetition. Video games employ all three . . . Violent games can deaden us to the horror of violence."

- What do you think? Do violent video games *teach* violent thinking and behavior? Explain.

- Have you seen media influence those around you for good or bad? Share examples, either positive or negative, about the influence of media.

- In your opinion, what should be off-limits for Christians when it comes to violent movies and video games? Is violence ever acceptable in the media we ingest as believers? Share your thoughts.

## ■ Reflect

Read Matthew 5:1–12, 38–48; 1 Corinthians 15:20–28. Take a few moments to jot down notes and observations. Is there any link between them? How do these passages compare/contrast? What questions do you have after reading them?

## ■ Let's Explore

### God's kingdom is one of peace.

*Blessed are the peacemakers. Turn the other cheek. The meek will inherit the earth. Love your enemies.* All phrases from Jesus's Sermon on the Mount. But are they any more than idealistic platitudes? We must allow Christ's words on meekness, mercy, peace, reconciliation, retaliation, and love for enemy inform our everyday actions. Even to the point of affecting our entertainment choices.

- What does Matthew 5:1–12, 38–48 tell you about God? about the values of his kingdom?

- How do these concepts differ from the values that are presented in popular film and video games? Share specific contrasting examples.

Though a case can easily be made berating the violence in today's culture, particularly its pervading and numbing presence in entertainment, Jesus's time and culture was also full of violence. It wasn't an idyllic, peaceful society he was speaking to—it was a culture in which public torture, brutal executions, violent revolutions, and threats of war were commonplace.

• How do Jesus's words speak to violence? Do you think he'd say anything different if he were speaking directly to us and to our culture? Explain.

• Do you think these standards Jesus set regarding peace and violence should be applied literally as the standard for the depictions of behavior that we should—or should not—watch? Or do you think there is a place for violence in our media choices as Christians? Explain.

• How can we cultivate the values and attitudes Jesus prescribes here in his sermon? How do you think violent media might affect the growth of, say, mercy and peacemaking in our lives?

"It shouldn't surprise us that all media shapes us, which is one reason Paul exhorts us to think on things that are true, honorable, pure, lovely, commendable, and excellent (Phil 4)," the editors of *Christianity Today* write.

- What could replace the violent images and values that flow through film and video games?

### God's kingdom will ultimately crush evil.

- What does 1 Corinthians 15:12–28 tell you about God? How would you summarize the thrust of this passage in your own words?

Verses 24–26 are not about Jesus, the meek and humble peacemaker; instead they paint Christ as the ultimate, victorious destroyer. Like this passage, there are many instances in Scripture in which God himself does things that are violent or destructive (or allows violence to occur) toward a good end.

- Name some Bible stories that come to mind in which violence is portrayed as a good (or morally neutral) thing. What's your reaction to the violence in those stories? What's your reaction to the picture of Christ as destroyer in 1 Corinthians 15?

We live in a world in which good and evil, right and wrong, are constantly battling—many times quite violently. This is reflected in the stories we immerse ourselves in, whether they be books, films, video games, or even sports. The *Christianity Today* editorial suggests that some violent stories can serve as "cathartic moral fiction" and even help us "construct a moral universe." We all have a desire for victory, for justice, for evil to be conquered. We can be encouraged by Scripture that God will put all his enemies under his feet (1 Cor. 15:25).

- Share some examples of stories in film or other forms of media that encourage you with their portrayal of the fight between good and evil. What do you most enjoy about these stories?

- In light of Christ's teachings on peace (in Matthew 5) and the biblical portrayals of violence you've just discussed, what do you think could be considered "appropriate" violence in film and video games? For example, is "killing" okay in a video game like *The Lord of the Rings: The Battle for Middle Earth* (based on the fictional tale by J.R.R. Tolkien) while it's not okay in a game portraying graphic gang violence like *Grand Theft Auto*? Why?

## ■ Going Forward

Form pairs to discuss these next two questions:

- How seriously have you taken Christ's teachings about peace? In what ways have you winked at the values of God's kingdom for the sake of indulging in violent entertainment?

- How do you feel you can demonstrate repentance? Are there specific changes you want to make in the way you approach violent entertainment? If so, what are they?

Gather back together as a group to discuss this final question:

Writer and painter Henry Miller once wrote,

Art is only a means to life, to the life more abundant. It is not in itself the life more abundant. It merely points the way, something which is overlooked not only by the public, but very often by the artist himself. In becoming an end it defeats itself.

The question here is if we use art—or entertainment—as a way of vicarious living rather than truly *living* our own lives. Could it be that we sometimes immerse ourselves in action hero films or first-person shooter games because they are more exciting or feel more satisfying than our own lives?

• What evil-conquering adventures may God be calling you to in real life?

As a group, pray for each others' goals in these areas. Recommit together to being adventurous kingdom citizens who value peace and mercy and the conquering of evil in this world.

# Can Christians influence the entertainment industry?

SCRIPTURE FOCUS

Matthew 5:13–16

1 John 2:15–17

# HOLLYWOOD DISCIPLES

■

It's not easy being salt and light in a place
better known for salty language and dark
content. So what does it take to be a follower
of Jesus in Tinseltown? The article "Creating the
Good in Hollywood" highlights the work of one such
Christian, Bryan Coley. Coley seeks to tread the fine
line of bringing biblical truth to secular entertainment
while maintaining a commitment to producing high
quality art. In this study we'll look at the role of
Christians in Hollywood and Christ's call to bring the
truth to our society, wherever we are.

## ■ Before You Meet

Read the article "Creating the Good in Hollywood."

# CREATING THE GOOD IN HOLLYWOOD

### Christian screenwriters are changing the film and television industries from the inside out.

*by LeAnne Benfield Martin*

Materialism. Drugs. Infidelity. Narcissism. When Christians talk about Hollywood, we usually shake our heads and go on about how terrible it is. Because it seems so blatantly anti-Christian, we've written it off rather than embraced it as the mission field it is.

At least two people, however, have caught God's vision for making a difference in Hollywood. While many in the church consider Hollywood hopeless, Bryan Coley and Barbara Nicolosi represent a growing movement of Tinseltown insiders who offer the hope of Christ.

### Sowing Seeds of Truth

Twelve years ago, Bryan Coley had season tickets to two Atlanta theater companies. The plays he saw glorified postmodernism and dysfunctional lives by depicting a "bunch of screwed-up people." But, he says, God tapped him on the shoulder and said, "You're just criticizing. You need to create."

A Christian all his life, Bryan started to feel guilty: the nonbelievers around him didn't have truth or hope. "Here I am, holding the Truth. How can I not express that?"

So in 1995 Bryan, a graduate of New York University's Tisch School of the Arts, started a writers' group. At first Art Within worked in the theater world, allowing Christian writers to grow artistically by getting their work on stage. Now, it commissions screenplays too. Its mission is to develop, produce, and distribute scripts relevant to contemporary culture that also explore Hope and Truth.

To that end, Bryan and his team developed Art Within Labs: a yearlong fellowship that allows a handful of writers to complete their screenplays.

The program culminates with staged readings at the annual Showcase and Symposium, a conference that brings together faith-based screenwriters, playwrights, and producers.

The labs and symposium grew out of Bryan's deep desire to change the world. "God is always moving before me and saying, 'Come on!' He's showing me the vision, and it's always about broken lives—a vision of what [those] lives can be."

But for the most part, the Christian community doesn't understand how to use Hollywood to touch broken people. "We need to be human beings, people who need a Savior, who need hope and truth. Although we found it, we need to understand what it's like not to have it."

Enter Bryan and Art Within, which acts as "a catalyst, sowing seeds to pave the way for what has to happen next." Sowing seeds in Hollywood means telling compelling stories with skill and artistry rather than trying to evangelize through poorly written work that gives Christ a bad name.

To reach nonbelievers, Bryan and his colleagues believe that Hollywood needs good stories that express dysfunction—a condition our culture knows well—but with Christ's grace, hope, and truth. "If you show beige against white, there's no contrast," says Bryan. "The Bible is all about showing red against white. It shows the Rahabs, the tax collectors, the sin.

"God didn't call us to be safe. He called us to share the Good News." With this in mind, the five writers in the labs are creating stories that offer mainstream appeal without holding back on the truth.

And Hollywood is watching. The success of films like *The Passion of the Christ* and *The Chronicles of Narnia* and the recent launch of FoxFaith Films have awakened Hollywood to the commercial power of the Christian market, but studios have no idea how to tap into this market. So, Bryan pitched them the stories from the labs, and studio executives plan to travel to Atlanta to hear the readings of those screenplays.

Bryan says the harvest is now. "God keeps telling me, 'Step up.' Every time I do, the doors fly open. At least for a time, He has given us the ear of the influential."

## Doing His Thing

"God is moving in Hollywood—that's so clear to me," says Barbara Nicolosi, screenwriter and co-editor of *Behind the Screen: Hollywood Insiders on Faith, Film, and Culture*. In 1999, Barbara and her colleagues started Act One, an educational outreach to writers of the Christian entertainment fellowship community, Inter-Mission. They saw a need for education because much of the work done by Christians was substandard.

"We were sick of the church's usual reaction to Hollywood, which is avoidance and boycott. That's not very pastoral," she says. "It's [easy] to demonize Hollywood. That's a simpler way to live: to blame Hollywood for all our problems." The result? "The church is keeping the good news to itself."

Meanwhile, "God is doing His thing." To help improve the work by Christians, Act One leaders teach an intense, four-week scriptwriting workshop, which includes everything a writer needs to know to enter the business of film and television in a professional way.

"Act One works," says Barbara, who chairs the group's board. Alumna Clare Sera, who began as a writers' assistant at DreamWorks, co-wrote *Curious George,* sold a movie to Paramount, and is developing a script with Art Within. Cheryl McKay wrote the screenplay for *The Ultimate Gift,* a feature film that hit theaters last fall. Other alums are scriptwriters for TV shows.

Breaking through takes time, but to Barbara it's worth it. "I love the industry and its potential to do good and to inspire." She wants people to consider movies a gift, to understand what they can do for the world.

"We need to be in the middle of the industry," she writes in *Behind the Screen*, "working side by side with those who do not share our worldview, so as to bring God where He is not."

With industry insiders like Barbara Nicolosi and Bryan Coley, there's hope for Hollywood yet.

---

*LeAnne Benfield Martin is a writer who lives in Georgia. "Creating the Good in Hollywood" was first published in* Today's Christian *July/August 2007, Ol. 45, No. 4, Page 34.*

# ■ Open Up

Select one of these activities to launch your discussion time.

## Option 1

Discuss these icebreaker questions:

- If you had the guarantee of at least moderate success, would you want a career in the entertainment industry? If so, what would you want to do? If not, why not?

- As a group, brainstorm together to identify any self-professed Christians in the entertainment industry. Were you able to come up with *more* or *fewer* names than you expected?

## Option 2

Bring several entertainment and celebrity magazines to the meeting. As a group, use glue and scissors to create a "This is Hollywood" collage. Simply go through the magazines and cut out images or words that you think best represent what Hollywood is all about. You can include both positive and negative ideas here—whatever you think represents the values and faces of the entertainment industry. When you're done, use your collage to discuss these questions:

- Can you imagine living and working in this culture? What (if anything) would you like about it?

- What are some of the temptations and challenges you think Christians in the entertainment industry face?

## ■ The Issue

Hollywood is arguably the most influential city in the world. New York is the world's economic center. Washington rules the political arena, but it is Hollywood that has captured the imaginations of people at every corner of the globe. American movies and television shows are seen in almost every country in the world. But the same entertainment machine that a few decades ago depicted the United States as the land of dreams today exports a steady stream of sex, graphic language, and violence.

In the middle of it all are a handful of Christians who are trying to make a living by writing decent, quality scripts that won't make their mothers blush—or grieve their Lord, for that matter. Some see themselves as screenwriters who happen to be Christians. Others know that, like it or not, they are covert missionaries.

- Jay Leno once said that "if God does not destroy Hollywood then he'll have to apologize to Sodom and Gomorrah." Is that an accurate assessment of the town and its stories? Why or why not?

- Do you think popular entertainment would be noticeably different if all the Christians quit working in the entertainment industry? Explain.

## ■ Reflect

Take a moment to read Matthew 5:13–16 and 1 John 2:15–17 on your own and jot down some notes. What common interpretations do people have for these passages? What words, phrases, or images jump out to you?

What connections do you see between these passages and entertainment? What questions do these passages raise for you?

# ■ Let's Explore

### Disciples influence their surroundings.

Early in his Sermon on the Mount, Jesus establishes the purpose his disciples will have in the world. First he gives several snapshots of his disciples. They are peacemakers; they are humble; they have no spiritual bragging rights; they are hungry for his righteousness. Then Jesus describes their effect on the world in the verses we are examining here. They are salt and light for a decaying and darkened society. In the remainder of the hillside sermon, Jesus gives examples of how this is lived out: what to do when you are angry, when you are tempted, when you are compelled to give up.

As we study the "salt and light" passage, consider the implications for Christians in show business. Ask how this text applies to any of us who have the opportunity to influence our society and to witness for Jesus Christ in places that are increasingly hostile to the gospel and those who want to share it.

Read Matthew 5:13–16.

Jesus tells ever-so-common listeners that they have great influence on the world. He calls them "salt." Salt for these hearers was probably sea salt, extracted by boiling vast amounts of ocean water until only the solids remained. Some of this salt's minerals were used as fertilizer. Salt was also one of the few disinfectants of the day, for household and medicinal use. "Rubbing salt in the wound" expresses something painful today, but Jesus's listeners understood that salt was a cleansing agent. Salt might hurt for a few minutes, but it promotes healing. And salt was mostly used as a food preservative, preventing or delaying decay. Without it, few vegetables and little meat could survive a winter. Without salt, many people would have gone hungry, and in desperate times, some might have died.

- Consider these roles: fertilizer, disinfectant, and preservative. How are Christians in places of influence acting like these things today?

- How could Christians in the entertainment industry function as salt in these three ways? Brainstorm specific examples.

- Which of these aspects of saltiness do you most focus on in your own life and in your own sphere of influence? Explain.

- Besides Hollywood, what are other areas of our culture in which Christians are trying to bring salt and light to people who seem hostile to gospel values? How can believers support Christians in these environments?

**Disciples spread the truth of the gospel.**

Jesus's second word-picture is a lamp. The gospel is the light that shines in the darkness of human need, and the followers of Christ are the bearers of that light. Just as an ancient city, often built of white limestone that gleamed in the sun, could not be hidden, so the gospel cannot be hidden. True disciples of Christ have a holy obligation to share the gospel, but that isn't easy in some settings.

According to Robert Johnston, professor of theology and culture at Fuller Theological Seminary and author of *Reel Spirituality*, there are three types of Christians in Hollywood:

— those who use the workplace as a forum for evangelism,

— those who bring biblical values and insight into the workplace, and

— those who see professional excellence as their calling and testimony to God.

"Which is right? All three," says Johnston. "There are evangelicals in Hollywood who would center their activity in each of those categories, but often when other Christians think of Christians in Hollywood, they're only thinking of the first category."

• Which of these three perspectives best represents the way you think Christians in the entertainment industry should approach their faith and work? Why?

• Consider your own work; which approach best matches how you see the interplay between your Christian faith and your workplace?

Ralph Winter, a Christian and a producer of films like *X-Men* and *Planet of the Apes*, said this in an interview with *Christianity Today*: "If you want to get into screenwriting because you want to convert people, it's the wrong reason." Winter believes a Christian screenwriter should focus more on crafting an excellent and compelling story rather than pushing an evangelistic message.

- Do you agree with Winter: that evangelism is the wrong reason to pursue screenwriting (or other aspects of the entertainment industry)? Or do you think Christians screenwriters *should* seek to produce evangelistic scripts? Explain.

- Is there a place in the believer's life for a silent witness, the kind represented by the view that excellence in the workplace is a testimony to God? Why or why not? If yes, give an example.

- What are some examples of great art—be it film, literature, or visual arts like painting—that you think draw people to God or communicate the gospel message? When have you personally been spiritually impacted by a work of art?

**Disciples face threats of dilution and darkness.**

Jesus warns his listeners that salt can lose its flavor and usefulness and that light can be hidden. In other words, careless disciples can lose their usefulness in the kingdom. If they do, they deserve only to be thrown out. Disciples who fulfill their purpose by living their faith publicly will cause others to praise God.

Theologian D. A. Carson summarizes: "If salt exercises the negative function of delaying and warns disciples of the danger of compromise and conformity to the world, then light speaks positively of illuminating a sin-darkened world and warns against withdrawal from the world that does not lead others to glorify the Father in heaven" (*Expositor's Bible Commentary*, Zondervan). Or, in the words of Dietrich Bonhoeffer, "A community of Jesus which seeks to hide itself has ceased to follow him."

- Are there "Christian" shows or movies you've seen that seemed to tread too lightly when it comes to sharing the gospel? Share your thoughts.

- Where would you be most tempted to compromise your faith if you worked in Hollywood?

- Do you think Christians who create shows and movies that depict immoral behavior, include curse words, or are violent are compromising their beliefs? Are they hiding their "light under a bowl" (Matthew 5:15)? Why or why not?

In 1 John, the believer is warned against setting his affections on the world and worldly things. The writer uses "world" to connote the polluted society and systems in which human beings live. In the article, the screenwriters live in a city and work in an industry that many would decry as a source of cultural pollution.

Read 1 John 2:15–17 again, but this time substitute "Hollywood" for "the world."

- Is this way of reading of 1 John 2:15–17 insightful? Or is it inaccurate? What's your take on how a Christian should love or guard against the entertainment industry?

- What threats of "dilution" do face in your own setting, occupation, or lifestyle? How can you guard against losing your saltiness?

## ■ Going Forward

- Based on what you've discussed so far, how would *you* define a Christian movie? Share examples of movies (or TV shows or books) that fit your definition.

- How have you felt inspired or challenged by Scripture and this discussion to live as salt and light in your workplace or community? In what ways do *you* desire to more boldly point others toward the truth?

Pray together for Christians in Hollywood and people in positions of influence. Pray about guarding your own heart.

It's the cry of our culture,

but is it compatible with

a life of faith?

SCRIPTURE FOCUS

Ecclesiastes 2:1–11

Colossians 3:12–17

# ENTERTAIN ME!

■

In the mid-1990s, the rock band Nirvana put their fingers on the pulse of American culture in their song "Smells Like Teen Spirit." The song's popular refrain proved to have a long shelf life: "Here we are now, entertain us," they repeated.

Their words embody much of our reality: the ways that we present ourselves to others, expecting to be entertained, and the rise of activities that can divert us from everything else in the world. As entertainment moves from exceptional to expected, Christians are required to consider anew how these shifts challenge our way of life and create new opportunities for faithfulness in our changing world.

Using "Is God Exciting Enough?"—Todd Hertz's *Christianity Today* interview with Richard Winter— we're going to dive into two questions: What does entertainment do to us? And how are we to respond?

## ■ Before You Meet

Read "Is God Exciting Enough?", Todd Hertz's interview with Richard Winter from *Christianity Today*.

# IS GOD EXCITING ENOUGH?

### The author of *Still Bored in a Culture of Entertainment* says that increased stimulation has caused a deadness of soul. What can turn it around?

*An interview with Richard Winter, by Todd Hertz*

In the foreword to his 1986 book, *Amusing Ourselves to Death*, Neil Postman suggested that the culture Aldous Huxley envisioned in *Brave New World* had become reality. "As [Huxley] saw it, people will come to love their oppression [and] to adore the technologies that undo their capacities to think," Postman wrote. "[What he] feared was that there would be no reason to ban a book, for there would be no one who wanted to read one." Postman argued that entertainment technologies had changed public discourse. As in *Brave New World*, Postman feared that an overload of information reduced culture to passivity and that truth was lost in irrelevance.

In the book *Still Bored in a Culture of Entertainment* (InterVarsity Press, 2002), author Richard Winter says that the same cultural occurrence has "seduced and brainwashed" people away from God. Todd Hertz, managing editor of Christianity Today International's *Ignite Your Faith* magazine, spoke with Winter, a professor of practical theology at Covenant Seminary, about how technology and exciting entertainment have created what he calls a "deadness of soul."

**What were you seeing in culture that you wanted to address?**

Everywhere I looked, I saw people using electronic entertainment. My children come home at night with, not just one video, but two or three. They also spend hours on end playing computer games with their friends. I began to wonder what effect this was having on them.

I explored the literature on boredom and came across this idea that overstimulation can lead to boredom as much as understimulation. People tend to lose the ability to develop their imagination and creativity because they're so dependent on input instead of producing something themselves.

In her book *Boredom: The Literary History of a State of Mind*, Patricia Meyer Spacks wrote that the word *boredom* came into the English language about 250 years ago. From then on, there has been an incredible rise in references to it in literature.

You will see that technology boomed in the same age. Access to greater technology increases at the same time that the use of the word *boredom* does in poetry and literature. People also now have much more leisure time at their disposal and shorter working days than they did back in the 1800s.

### How does your theory differ from what Neil Postman argues?

It's very much the same. His book title is so great: *Amusing Ourselves to Death*. I have very similar themes, but I place it in the Christian context because the decline of Christianity is a very significant factor in all of this. There's a parallel between the rise of these incidences of boredom and the decline of Christianity, faith, and spirituality.

### Does the lack of faith cause boredom, or has more boredom created a lack of faith?

I think it's a little bit of both. There's a vicious circle—a deadness of soul leads to boredom, and boredom, of course, leads to deadness of soul.

Someone who is not a Christian [will experience this deadness of soul] because they're cut off completely from God and from any bigger sense of purpose and reality. On the other hand, when a Christian becomes jaded and feels that God is far away, this person gets bored with prayer and with Bible study. He or she then feels a certain deadness of soul as well.

[The problem] comes down to a loss of a bigger picture of life that, for a Christian, would give significance to all the small details of life. As

I wash the dishes, work in the garden, or vacuum, I see it in the context of both the commitment to my relationship with my wife and my family, but also as a commitment to God that I'm called to do these things. And Christ should be Lord of every detail of my life. The seemingly boring, mundane things have a much greater significance in the big picture if you live with faith.

### In this culture, is God exciting enough?

We're so dependent on things being exciting. Even as I listen to people giving announcements in church—especially for the youth—everything has got to be really exciting to grab their attention. There's a danger in our worship services when we try to become entertaining.

It's of course good to use illustrations, variety, visual aids, and so on, but one can go over the top so that it just becomes another theatrical production to give people a good feeling, which they then may mistake for an experience of God. But really it's just generated by the sort of entertainment.

God occasionally does amazing, wonderful, and miraculous things. But most of the time, it is the ordinary things of life that he works through. I think our dependence on this sort of hyperstimulation and busyness makes it very hard for us to be content with the small things, with the quieter moments.

### How does this hurt a Christian's personal relationship with God?

Overstimulation has led to a culture that has difficulties with delayed gratification. We want things now. We want instant spirituality and an instant relationship with God. Most of the giants of the faith talk about the slow, steady, day-by-day walk of obedience in faith without much drama and with the need for discipline.

The dependence on electronic entertainment doesn't help us to do the hard work of daily practice. If someone wants to play the piano, but they want to do it instantly and they don't have patience, they get too bored with daily exercises on the piano. Our spiritual life is a bit like that. I struggle with this too, to sit still in the presence of God and to read the Scriptures, to meditate, to pray. It's hard. I want to be up, busy, and active.

I was speaking to someone just yesterday who said that he cannot stand the ordinariness of life. He wants action. He wants all of God, or nothing. He wants God to come down and give him a big hug and make him feel wonderful, or he doesn't want anything to do with God.

This culture also hurts your relationships with other people and with nature. The real world, the natural world, runs at a slower pace. Things are more gentle than the drama of the electronic entertainment.

I went to see the new James Bond film the other day, and it's a classic example of how excitement begets more excitement. The color, the sound, the action, all is up several notches from previous ones to keep people's attention. How long can you go on like this?

**How can we battle this overstimulation, not only in our own lives, but also to the people we minister to?**

It's about building relationships rather than having exciting events. It's in the context of relationships that we make the most significant movement and growth in life. Even though high drama events sometimes produce results, they often don't last very long.

That's the other thing that technology has done. It's given us lots of wonderful things, but it's helped to undermine community because we don't need to sit on the porch and we have all our entertainment inside on the screen. Entertainment also undermines community in the family because each person sits in front of their own screen. Or you all sit in front of the screen together but you don't talk to each other. So in every way, technology cuts us off from relationships and from reality.

Television suggests that life is high drama, love, and sex. Activities such as housework, fundraising, and teaching children to read are vastly underreported. Most pleasures are small pleasures—a hot shower, a sunset, a bowl of good soup, or a good book.

*Richard Winter is professor of practical theology and head of the counseling program at Covenant Theological Seminary; he is the author of several books including* Still Bored in a Culture of Entertainment. *Todd Hertz is managing editor of Christianity Today International's* Ignite Your Faith *magazine. "Is God Exciting Enough" was first published online by* Christianity Today *on January 1, 2003.*

# ■ Open Up

Select one of these activities to launch your discussion time.

## Option 1

Discuss these icebreaker questions:

- Think of a time **when** you were entertained by something **other than** electronic media (such as viewing a live performance, observing children, and so on.) Describe what was positive and enjoyable about that entertainment experience.

- Which do you prefer: entertainment from electronic media (such as movies, TV shows, or video games) or non-electronic entertainment (such as books, playing musical instruments, board games, and so on)? Why? Which of these forms of entertainment is most often a part of your life?

- Brainstorm two quick "top **three**" lists as a group: What are the top **three** positive aspects of entertainment in our lives? And second: What are the top **three** negative results of entertainment in our lives?

## Option 2

One of the standout characteristics of entertainment is how effectively it saturates almost any situation we are in. Take five minutes as a group and count all the forms of entertainment in the building (or room) in which you're meeting. Write down all the different kinds of distractions or sources of entertainment that you count. Review your list together, then talk about these questions:

- Were you surprised by the amount of forms of entertainment you came up with? Why or why not?

- What do you see as the main effects, positive or negative, of having so many forms of entertainment so close at hand?

# ■ The Issue

- Spiritually speaking, do you view entertainment as good, bad, or neutral? Explain your point of view.

Entertainment is not a bad thing. In Ecclesiastes, the Teacher commends us to enjoy ourselves, saying, "So go eat your food and enjoy it; drink your wine and be happy, because that is what God wants you to do" (Eccl. 9:7). But unlike Solomon's generation, we don't live in a world in which entertainment is a rare event in an otherwise difficult existence. Central in many homes (even bedrooms) is a television set, and many of us plan our schedules around season premieres and opening nights.

The people who create and sell entertainment know their audiences—us. They know what makes our eyes open wide, our pulses race, our jaws drop. They know how to entice us and keep us coming back.

It's hard to read the Bible when action and intrigue are only a few button-pushes away. It's difficult to commit to a life of discipleship when our culture turns out visions of action-packed lives filled with drama and excitement. Since Christians believe, however, that discipleship plays out over the course of an entire life, we need to develop guards against the attitude that entertainment portrays to us the real "stuff" of life. Instead, we need to live as though God's love for us—demonstrated to us in manners big and small—is the best way to live.

- When have you personally experienced tension between your desire to be entertained (or your attachment to a particular form of entertainment) and the callings and demands of your faith in Christ?

# ■ Reflect

Read Ecclesiastes 2:1–11 and Colossians 3:12–17 on your own. Jot down some notes about your observations. How does each passage cast a vision for how we are to live our lives? What lessons rise to the surface that apply to the types of entertainment we pursue? What challenges you personally in these passages?

# ■ Let's Explore

### Entertainment can numb us to the world and the experiences around us.

In his interview with Todd Hertz, author and professor Richard Winter said, "Overstimulation has led to culture that has difficulties with delayed gratification . . . I went to see the new James Bond film the other day, and it's a classic example of how excitement begets excitement . . . How long can you go on like this?"

- How have you experienced the truths of Winter's statement? When have you felt overstimulated by a movie, TV show, or other form of entertainment?

King Solomon, the "Teacher" of Ecclesiastes, lived his life blessed with wisdom and power. Every door in the ancient world was open to him: he could have any object (or person) he desired. Ecclesiastes records a time in Solomon's life in which he applied himself to understanding wisdom and knowledge (1:17). The first item on his agenda of things to explore: pleasure.

Read Ecclesiastes 2:4–9, the record of Solomon's self-centered life.

• Which of the pleasures Solomon recounts translates directly into the world of entertainment that our culture produces? Give examples.

• Winter believes that we are too dependent on excitement and that we suffer because the media trains us to expect all of life to bring us deep emotions and dramatic events. Do you agree or disagree? Why?

• In Ecclesiastes 2:10–11, the Teacher gives his report on the pleasure he sought: Useless! Meaningless! Vanity! Do you think his words resonate with people who are, as Winter would say, "overstimulated" by entertainment? Have you ever felt this way after watching a movie or some other form of entertainment? Explain.

God wants us to enjoy life, including the aspects that are "regular" and mundane.

Paul's letter to the Colossians is meant for a fellowship of people who are living life together. In chapter 3, Paul turns his attention to the ins-and-outs of "regular" life for his friends in Asia Minor (what is now Turkey).

- Read Colossians 3:12–17. Focus on verse 12 and look at the five characteristics Paul tells his readers to take up. How important are those characteristics in your relationships? How does their priority in your life compare to their prevalence in popular entertainments?

Winter says: "The dependence on electronic entertainment doesn't help us to do the hard work of daily practice . . . I struggle with this too, to sit still in the presence of God and to read the Scriptures, to meditate, to pray. It's hard. I want to be up, busy, and active."

- Does that statement hit close to home for you? Share from your own experience.

Forming habits of continually being entertained can lead to a self-centered view of the world. We can find ourselves responding to relationships, responsibilities at work, or even sermons with a mind-set that says, "This doesn't do much for me" or "I don't get a lot out of this." In other words, we aren't entertained enough . . . we're left bored, unsatisfied, or understimulated. But the focus here can be summed up in three words: me, me, me. Colossians 3, on the other hand, portrays an others-focused view of life.

- Do you agree with the notion that our entertainment culture breeds self-centeredness? If so, how have you seen this creeping into the church? If you don't agree, explain your rationale.

Almost all of Colossians 3 is written in the plural (so, we could substitute "you" with "you all" to hear the words as the first readers heard them). The chapter as a whole presents a portrait of Christian life—life characterized by mutual service, accountability, and encouragement.

- How does this image of the Christian life contrast with Winter's entertainment- and technology-driven image of our culture?

- What are some of the things you enjoy about life that aren't celebrated in our entertainment culture? How have you seen God in the small things in life that may not be the substance of a movie but that are deeply meaningful all the same?

## ■ Going Forward

Discuss the following quote and questions as a group.

In defense of entertainment, pastor and film festival director David Taylor once wrote: "[Movies and entertainment] remind us to live from the heart, not from dutifulness. They remind us that, at the end of the day, God does not need our little productivities."

The bad thing about entertainment, as the German poet Rainer Maria Rilke put it, is not our acceptance of it but a tendency to "misuse and squander this experience as a stimulant at the tired spots" of our lives and as a distraction, instead of as a lightening of the spirit (ChristianityTodayMovies.com, July, 2004).

- What are some ways we can help each other avoid turning to entertainment "as a stimulant at the tired spots"?

- What are the areas in which entertainment risks making you numb to the events in your world and, especially, in your spiritual life?

- What guidelines can we put in place to make sure we don't get too caught up in the overstimulation of entertainment?

Now form pairs and pray together about entertainment's role in each of your lives. Consider how it influences your view on life's more mundane aspects—relationships, personal devotions, service to others. Ask God to help you each think critically about entertainment, so that as you use your leisure time, you won't be damaging your ability to participate in the unglamorous aspects of the Christian life. Instead, as you take time out to enjoy yourself, you'll be glorifying God by enjoying the reality that, in Taylor's words, "God doesn't need our little productivities."

2/3
■ **Notes**

John— nephew Jacob ~ repeating 8th
       grade ~ and his mom's in
       and out of jail
    — Lifesavers Fellowship
      — sci fi convention

Linda  to get home safe Sat.

allison — hernia operation in
    March / can't  begin job yet
    one place  willing  to hold job

**Liz**'s  boss — has had  a
(Wendy)  hard year — grieving, job chang
           wisdom about
Bob — involvement in new campa

Mario — Paul expecting baby / looking fo
       Jennabel — new job / mentorin

Megan — long work days, much stress
    — endurance

eghan - work
rin - brother w/ cancer
new - ☒

■ Notes       3 | 3

─ convention
✳ John ─ Jacob & his mother

Linda & Nate
Jen & Mario        } BABIES !!

Todd ─ mom's gallbladder
Tara    (Dee)   surgery

Mario ─ heartburn every day
Liz ─ brother in afghanistan ─
          safety ─ Daniel

Damian ─ asthma
Grandma , Courtney appts
Linda's mom ─ gallbladder recovery
Bob ─ looking forward, calm
                  spirit

Ted ─ praise─ that growth in
      breast didn't worsen grow
Nate ─ new campus launch
      Allison had hernia surgery,
         recuperation
① Jill ─ Terry having baby on bed rest
      ─ issues at work

127

Jennabel ~ mentoring relationship

Nate - new campus care coordinator

Damian - friend's (Tiffany) working
relationship w/ boss ~
or new job

Liz - brother @ Daniel in
Afghanistan

Ali - back injury, job
interview
Thurs.

Linda - sister Carla
breakup -
peace - comfort

Ted -

John = friend Roy who's going to be
military chaplain @
# who's in basic training -
to do physical requirements
- sci fi ministry ...?

Bob - focus on @ sewing as God
wants him to

Megan - coworker whose grandfather passed
(email) away
- Megan & Duane
job pile up after ski
trip